THE EASY 4-CHORD FAKE BOOK

Melody, Lyrics and Simplified Chords

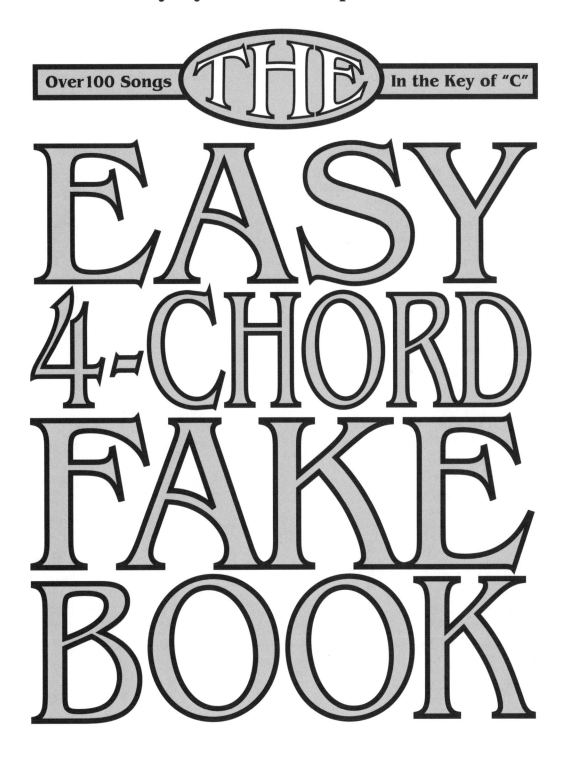

Over 100 Songs — THE — In the Key of "C"

THE EASY 4-CHORD FAKE BOOK

ISBN 978-1-4803-4004-6

HAL•LEONARD®
CORPORATION

7777 W. BLUEMOUND RD. P.O. BOX 13819 MILWAUKEE, WI 53213

Visit Hal Leonard Online at
www.halleonard.com

THE EASY 4-CHORD FAKE BOOK

CONTENTS

4 INTRODUCTION

6 **Act Naturally**
Buck Owens, The Beatles

8 **Back Home Again**
John Denver

14 **Beast of Burden**
The Rolling Stones

5 **Bei Mir Bist Du Schön**
(Means That You're Grand)
The Andrews Sisters

18 **Born to Be Wild**
Steppenwolf

20 **Brown Eyed Girl**
Van Morrison

22 **Candle in the Wind**
Elton John

26 **Catch the Wind**
Donovan

28 **Do Wah Diddy Diddy**
Manfred Mann

11 **Don't Be Cruel**
(To a Heart That's True)
Elvis Presley

25 **Don't Stop**
Fleetwood Mac

30 **Down Under**
Men at Work

32 **Drift Away**
Dobie Gray, Uncle Kracker

35 **Every Rose Has Its Thorn**
Poison

38 **Fields of Gold**
Sting

43 **Forever and Ever, Amen**
Randy Travis

40 **Forever Young**
Rod Stewart

46 **Free Ride**
Edgar Winter Group

48 **Fun, Fun, Fun**
The Beach Boys

50 **Garden Song**
John Denver

52 **Girls Just Want to Have Fun**
Cyndi Lauper

54 **Go Your Own Way**
Fleetwood Mac

56 **Good Riddance (Time of Your Life)**
Green Day

58 **A Groovy Kind of Love**
The Mindbenders, Phil Collins

60 **Have You Ever Seen the Rain?**
Creedence Clearwater Revival

62 **Hey, Good Lookin'**
Hank Williams

64 **Hey, Soul Sister**
Train

68 **How to Save a Life**
The Fray

74 **I Feel Fine**
The Beatles

76 **I Heard It Through the Grapevine**
Gladys Knight & The Pips, Marvin Gaye

78 **I Knew You Were Trouble.**
Taylor Swift

82 **I Love How You Love Me**
The Paris Sisters, Bobby Vinton

84 **I Shot the Sheriff**
Eric Clapton

73 **I'd Like to Teach the World to Sing**
The New Seekers, The Hillside Singers

86 **I'm a Believer**
The Monkees

88 **I've Just Seen a Face**
The Beatles

90 **If I Had a Hammer (The Hammer Song)**
Peter, Paul & Mary; Trini Lopez

92 **If I Were a Carpenter**
Bobby Darin

94 **It Never Rains in Southern California**
Albert Hammond

91 **It's a Small World**
*from Disneyland Resort® and
Magic Kingdom® Park*

96 **Jessie's Girl**
Rick Springfield

102 **Jimmy Mack**
Martha & The Vandellas

99 **Kiss the Girl**
from The Little Mermaid

104 **Knock Three Times**
Dawn

106 **Knockin' on Heaven's Door**
Bob Dylan

107 **Last Kiss**
J. Frank Wilson, Pearl Jam

110 **Learning to Fly**
Tom Petty & The Heartbreakers

114 **Let Her Cry**
Hootie & The Blowfish

113 **Let's Get Together (Get Together)**
The Youngbloods

116 **Little Sister**
Elvis Presley, Dwight Yoakam

120 **Lookin' Out My Back Door**
Creedence Clearwater Revival

122 **Love Stinks**
J. Geils Band

119 **Massachusetts (The Lights Went Out)**
Bee Gees

124 **Memories Are Made of This**
Dean Martin, Gale Storm

126 **Mr. Tambourine Man**
Bob Dylan, The Byrds

128 **The Night They Drove Old Dixie Down**
Joan Baez

130 **Octopus's Garden**
The Beatles

134 **One Love**
Bob Marley

136 **Peaceful Easy Feeling**
Eagles

138 **Peggy Sue**
Buddy Holly

144 **Pink Houses**
John Cougar Mellencamp

146 **Please Mr. Postman**
The Marvelettes, Carpenters

150 **Put a Little Love in Your Heart**
Jackie DeShannon

133 **Red, Red Wine**
Neil Diamond, UB40

152 **Run Around**
Blues Traveler

141 **Runaround Sue**
Dion & The Belmonts

156 **Should I Stay or Should I Go**
The Clash

162 **So You Want to Be a
Rock and Roll Star**
The Byrds

159 **Somebody to Love**
Jefferson Airplane

167 **Southern Cross**
Crosby, Stills & Nash

170 **Spanish Eyes**
Al Martino

164 **Sparks Fly**
Taylor Swift

172 **Spooky**
Classics IV

174 **Stand by Me**
Ben E. King

179 **Stayin' Alive**
Bee Gees

176 **Stuck in the Middle with You**
Stealers Wheel

182 **Sundown**
Gordon Lightfoot

184 **Supercalifragilisticexpialidocious**
from Mary Poppins

186 **Surfin' Safari**
The Beach Boys

188 **Susie-Q**
Creedence Clearwater Revival

189 **Suzanne**
Leonard Cohen, Judy Collins

192 **Sweet Home Alabama**
Lynyrd Skynyrd

194 **Sweet Jane**
Lou Reed, Cowboy Junkies

196 **A Teenager in Love**
Dion & The Belmonts

198 **That'll Be the Day**
The Crickets

200 **This Magic Moment**
Jay & The Americans

202 **The Times They Are A-Changin'**
Bob Dylan

207 **Today Was a Fairytale**
Taylor Swift

210 **Toes**
Zac Brown Band

214 **Turn the Page**
Bob Seger, Metallica

204 **Two Princes**
Spin Doctors

219 **Walking in the Sunshine**
Roger Miller

216 **Wanted Dead or Alive**
Bon Jovi

223 **The Way You Do the Things You Do**
The Temptations

220 **Wide Open Spaces**
Dixie Chicks

224 **Wild Thing**
The Troggs

226 **Wonderful Tonight**
Eric Clapton

228 **The Wreck of the Edmund Fitzgerald**
Gordon Lightfoot

230 **You Didn't Have to Be So Nice**
The Lovin' Spoonful

232 **You're Still the One**
Shania Twain

234 **Your Cheatin' Heart**
Hank Williams

236 **CHORD SPELLER**

INTRODUCTION

What Is a Fake Book?

A fake book has one-line music notation consisting of melody, lyrics and chord symbols. This lead sheet format is a "musical shorthand" which is an invaluable resource for all musicians—hobbyists to professionals.

Here's how *The Easy 4-Chord Fake Book* differs from most standard fake books:

- All songs are in the key of C.

- Only three basic chord types are used—major, minor and seventh.

- The music notation is larger for ease of reading.

In the event that you haven't used chord symbols to create accompaniment, or your experience is limited, a chord speller chart is included at the back of the book to help you get started.

Have fun!

BEI MIR BIST DU SCHÖN
(Means That You're Grand)

Original Words by JACOB JACOBS
Music by SHOLOM SECUNDA
English Version by SAMMY CAHN and SAUL CHAPLIN

ACT NATURALLY

Words and Music by VONIE MORRISON
and JOHNNY RUSSELL

Moderately

They're gon - na put me in the mov - ies. _____
make the scene a - bout a man that's sad and lone - ly, _____

_____ They're gon - na make a big star out of
_____ and beg - gin' down up - on his bend - ed

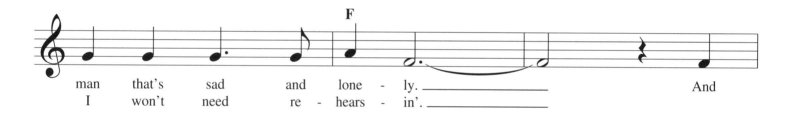

me. We'll make a film a - bout a
knee. I'll play the part, but

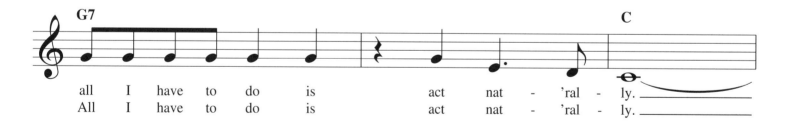

man that's sad and lone - ly. _____ And
I won't need re - hears - in'. _____

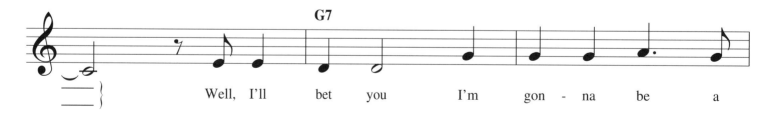

all I have to do is act nat - 'ral - ly. _____
All I have to do is act nat - 'ral - ly. _____

Well, I'll bet you I'm gon - na be a
big star. _____ Might win an Os - car,

BACK HOME AGAIN

Words and Music by
JOHN DENVER

There's a storm __ a - cross the val - ley, __ clouds are roll - in' in. __

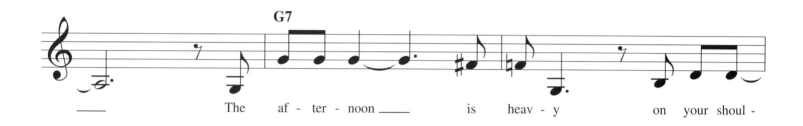

__ The af - ter - noon __ is heav - y on your shoul -

- ders. __ There's a truck out on __ the four __

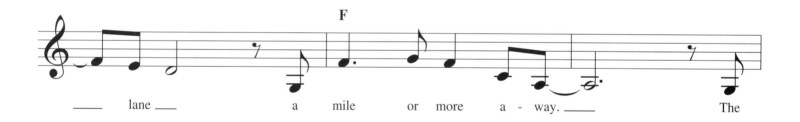

__ lane __ a mile or more a - way. __ The

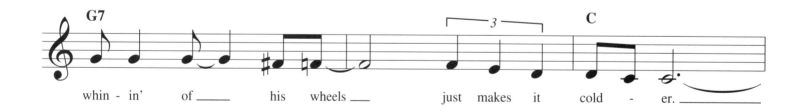

whin - in' of __ his wheels __ just makes it cold - er. __

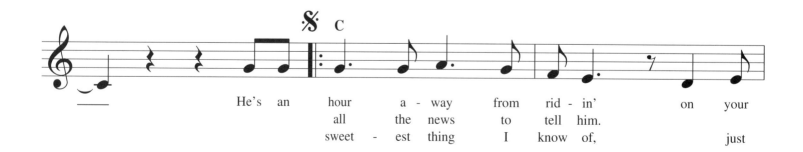

He's an hour a - way from rid - in' on your
all the news to tell him.
sweet - est thing I know of,   just

F
3
G7
prayers up in the sky; and ten days on the road
How'd you spend your time? And what's the lat - est thing
spend - in' time with you. It's the lit - tle things that make
C
are bare - ly gone. There's a
the neigh - bors say? And your
a house a home, like a
F
fire soft - ly burn - ing, sup - per's on the stove.
moth - er called last Fri - day; "Sun - shine" made her cry,
fire soft - ly burn - ing and sup - per on the stove
G7
But it's the light in your eyes that makes him
and you felt the ba - by move just yes - ter -
and the light in your eyes that makes me
C
Fine
F
warm.
day.
warm.
Hey, it's good to
G7
C
F
be back home a - gain. Some - times

DON'T BE CRUEL
(To a Heart That's True)

Words and Music by OTIS BLACKWELL
and ELVIS PRESLEY

Brightly

You know I can be found
Ba - by, if I made you mad for

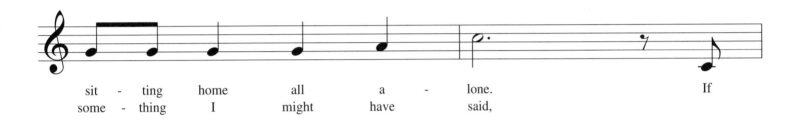

sit - ting home all a - lone.   If
some - thing I might have said,

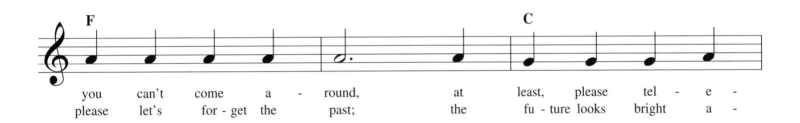

you can't come a - round,   at least, please tel - e -
please let's for - get the past;   the fu - ture looks bright a -

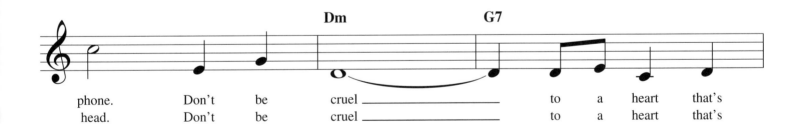

phone.   Don't be cruel _____ to a heart that's
head.   Don't be cruel _____ to a heart that's

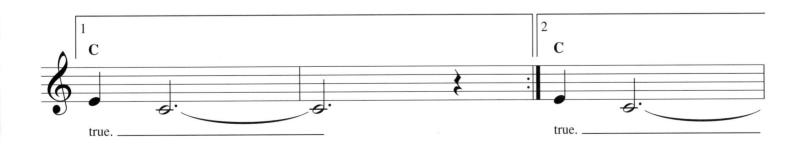

1
C
true. _____

2
C
true. _____

BEAST OF BURDEN

Words and Music by MICK JAGGER
and KEITH RICHARDS

Slow beat

I'll nev-er be your beast ___ of bur-den. My back is broad, ___
I'll nev-er be your beast ___ of bur-den. I've walked for miles, ___

but it's a-hurt-ing. All I want is for you to make love to me. ___
my feet are hurt-ing. All I want is for you to make love to me. ___

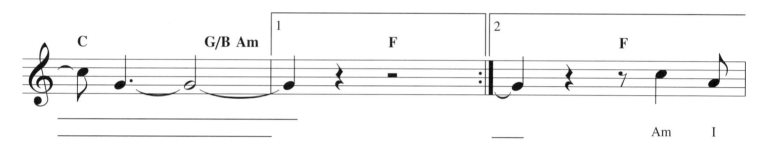

___ Am I

hard e-nough? ___ Am I rough e-nough? ___ Am I rich e-nough? ___ I'm

not too blind ___ to see ___ I'll nev-er be your beast ___

___ of bur-den. So let's go home ___ and draw the cur-tains,

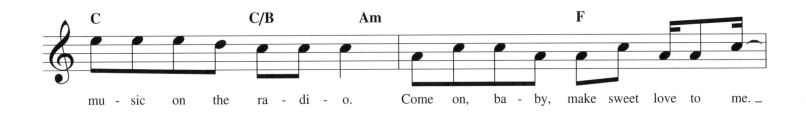

music on the ra - di - o. Come on, ba - by, make sweet love to me. ___

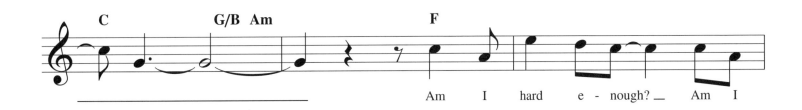

Am I hard e - nough? ___ Am I

rough e - nough? ___ Am I rich e - nough? ___ I'm not too blind ___ to see. ___

___ Oh, lit - tle sis - ter, _____ pret - ty, pret - ty,

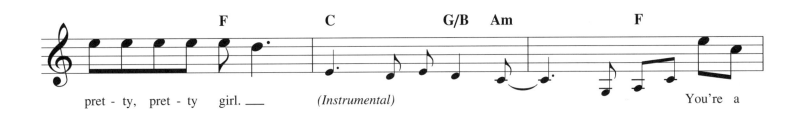

pret - ty, pret - ty girl. ___ *(Instrumental)* You're a

pret - ty, pret - ty, pret - ty, pret - ty, pret - ty, pret - ty girl. ___ Pret - ty, pret - ty, such a pret - ty,

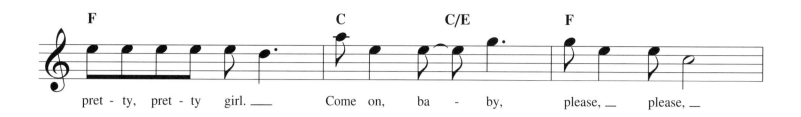

pret - ty, pret - ty girl. ___ Come on, ba - by, please, ___ please, ___

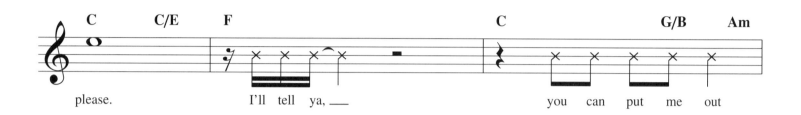

please. I'll tell ya, ___ you can put me out

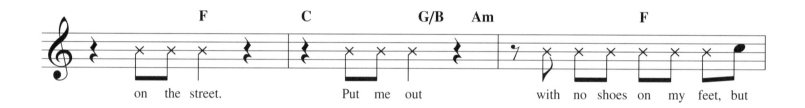

on the street. Put me out with no shoes on my feet, but

put me out, put me out, put me out of mis - er - y, _____

yeah. All your sick - ness, I can suck it up.

Throw it all at me, I can shrug it off. There's one thing that

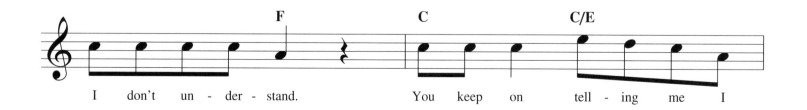

I don't un - der - stand. You keep on tell - ing me I

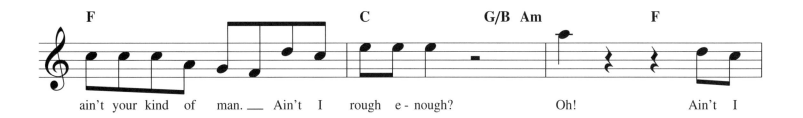

ain't your kind of man. ___ Ain't I rough e - nough?   Oh!   Ain't I

tough e - nough?   Ain't I rich e - nough, in love e - nough?

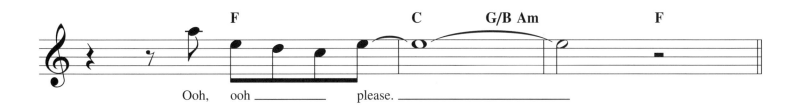

Ooh, ooh _____ please. _____

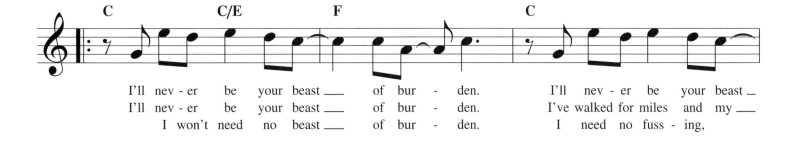

I'll nev - er be your beast ___ of bur - den.   I'll nev - er be your beast ___
I'll nev - er be your beast ___ of bur - den.   I've walked for miles and my ___
I won't need no beast ___ of bur - den.   I need no fuss - ing,

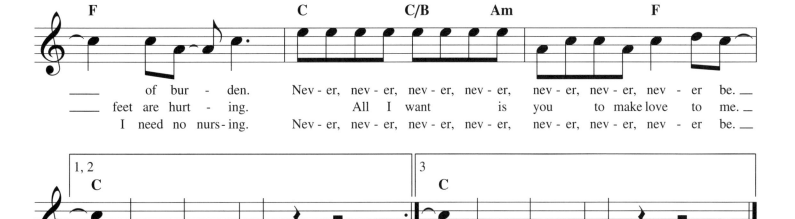

___ of bur - den.   Nev - er, nev - er, nev - er, nev - er,   nev - er, nev - er, nev - er be. ___
___ feet are hurt - ing.   All I want is you to make love to me. ___
I need no nurs - ing.   Nev - er, nev - er, nev - er, nev - er,   nev - er, nev - er, nev - er be. ___

1, 2   3
C   C

BORN TO BE WILD

Words and Music by
MARS BONFIRE

Moderate Rock beat

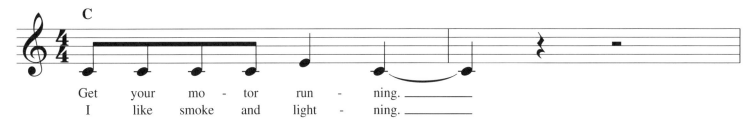

Get your mo - tor run - ning. _____
I like smoke and light - ning. _____

Head out on the high - way _____   look - ing for ad - ven - ture
Heav - y met - al thun - der _____   rac - ing in the wind

in what - ev - er comes our way. _____
and the feel - ing that I'm un - der. _____

Yeah, dar - ling, gon - na make it hap - pen,

take the world in a love em - brace. __   Fire __ all of your guns __

BROWN EYED GIRL

Words and Music by
VAN MORRISON

Moderately fast

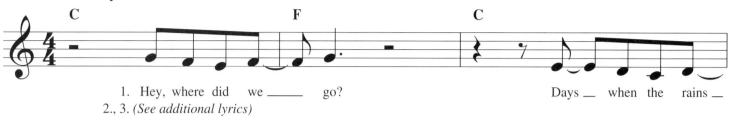

1. Hey, where did we _____ go? Days _____ when the rains _____
2., 3. *(See additional lyrics)*

_____ came, down _____ in the hol - low

play - in' a new _____ game, laugh - ing and a -

run - ning, hey, _____ hey, skip - ping and a - jump - ing.

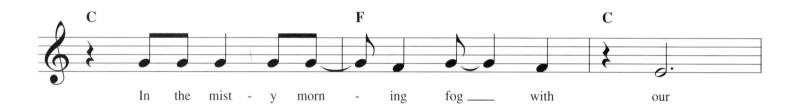

In the mist - y morn - ing fog _____ with our

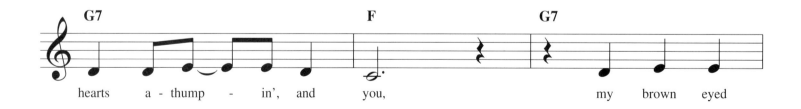

hearts a - thump - in', and you, my brown eyed

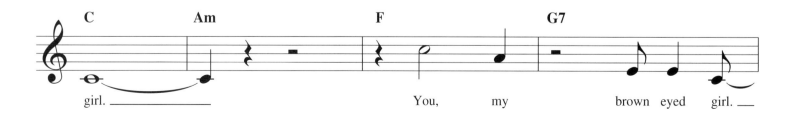

girl. _____ You, my brown eyed girl. _____

Do you re-mem - ber when

Chorus

we used to sing: ___ sha la ___ la la ___ la la ___ la la ___

___ la la la te da. ___ Sha la ___ la la ___

___ la la ___ la la ___ la la la te da ___ la te da. ___

Additional Lyrics

2. Whatever happened to Tuesday and so slow
   Going down the old mine with a transistor radio
   Standing in the sunlight laughing
   Hiding behind a rainbow's wall
   Slipping and a-sliding
   All along the waterfall
   With you, my brown eyed girl
   You, my brown eyed girl.
   Do you remember when we used to sing:
   Chorus

3. So hard to find my way, now that I'm all on my own
   I saw you just the other day, my, how you have grown
   Cast my memory back there, Lord
   Sometime I'm overcome thinking 'bout
   Making love in the green grass
   Behind the stadium
   With you, my brown eyed girl
   With you, my brown eyed girl.
   Do you remember when we used to sing:
   Chorus

CANDLE IN THE WIND

Words and Music by ELTON JOHN
and BERNIE TAUPIN

Moderate Ballad

Good-bye, Nor - ma Jean. _____ Though I nev - er knew you _____ at all, _____
Lone - li - ness _____ was tough, _____ the tough-est role you ev - er played. _

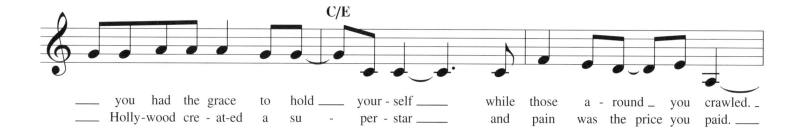

_____ you had the grace to hold _____ your - self _____ while those a - round _ you crawled. _
_____ Holly-wood cre - at-ed a su - per - star _____ and pain was the price you paid. _____

They crawled out of the wood -work and they whis-pered
And e - ven when you died, oh, the press

in - to _____ your brain. _____ They sent you _ on a tread - mill and they
still hound - ed you. _____ All the pa - pers had _____ to say was that

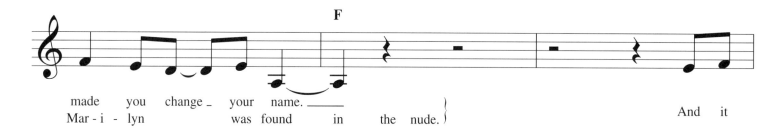

made you change _ your name. _____
Mar - i - lyn was found in the nude. }
And it

seems to me _____ you lived your life _____ like a can - dle in _____ the wind, _

nev - er know-ing who ___ to cling ___ to when the rain ___

_____ set in. ___ And I would ___ have liked ___ to have known

you but I was just _____ a kid. Your can - dle burned __ out

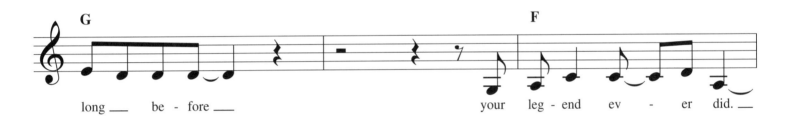

long __ be - fore ___ your leg - end ev - er did. __

To Coda ⊕

_____ (Instrumental)

Good - bye, Nor - ma Jean. ___ Though I nev - er

knew you __ at all, _____ you had the grace to hold ___ your - self ___ while

those a - round __ you crawled. __ Good bye, Nor - ma Jean, __

__ from a young man in the twen - ty - sec - ond row _____ who sees you as some-thing more __

__ than sex - ual, __ more than just our Mar - i - lyn ____ Mon - roe. And it

I would have liked __ to known you, oh, __ but I __

__ was just a kid. Your can - dle burned __ out long _____ be - fore _____

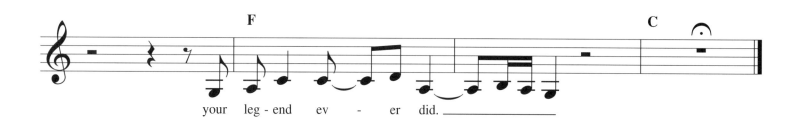

your leg - end ev - er did. _____

DON'T STOP

Words and Music by
CHRISTINE McVIE

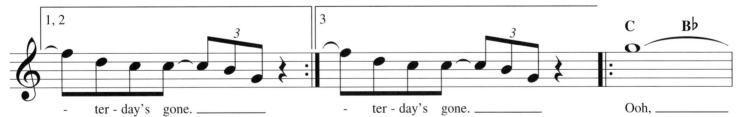

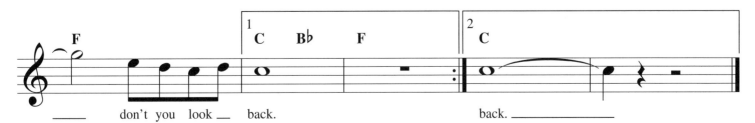

CATCH THE WIND

Words and Music by
DONOVAN LEITCH

Flowing

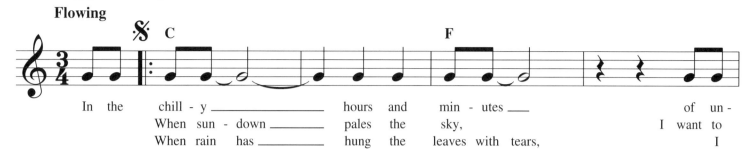

In the chill - y _____ hours and min - utes _____ of un -
When sun - down _____ pales the sky, I want to
When rain has _____ hung the leaves with tears, I

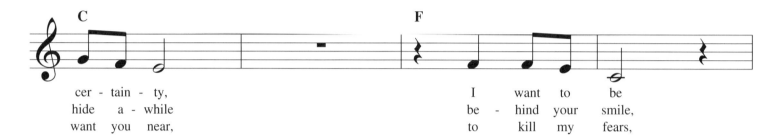

cer - tain - ty, I want to be
hide a - while be - hind your smile,
want you near, to kill my fears,

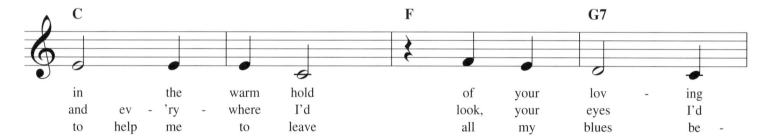

in the warm hold of your lov - ing
and ev - 'ry - where I'd look, your your eyes I'd
to help me to leave all my blues be -

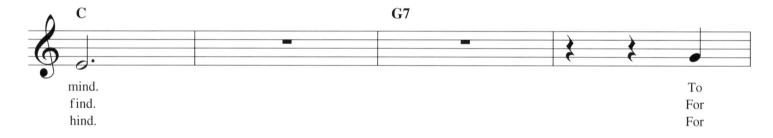

mind. To
find. For
hind. For

feel you _____ all a - round me and to
me to _____ love you now would be the
stand - ing _____ in your heart is where

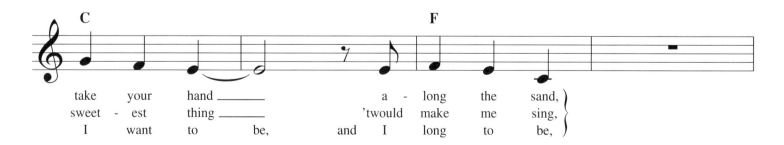

take your hand _____ a - long the sand,
sweet - est thing _____ 'twould make me sing,
I want to be, and I long to be,

DO WAH DIDDY DIDDY

Words and Music by JEFF BARRY
and ELLIE GREENWICH

Moderately fast

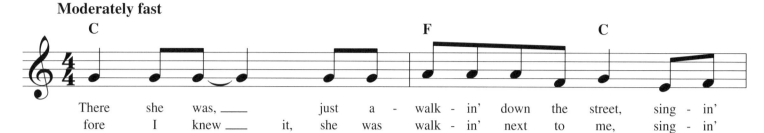

There she was, _____ just a - walk - in' down the street, sing - in'
fore I knew _____ it, she was walk - in' next to me, sing - in'

do wah did - dy did - dy, dum did - dy do.
do wah did - dy did - dy, dum did - dy do.

Snap - pin' her fin - gers and a - shuf - fl - in' her feet, sing - in'
Hold - in' my hand _____ just as nat - 'ral as can be, sing - in'

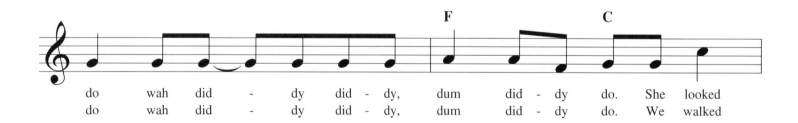

do wah did - dy did - dy, dum did - dy do. She looked
do wah did - dy did - dy, dum did - dy do. We walked

good (looked good), she looked fine (looked fine). She looked good, she looked fine, and I
on (walked on) to my door (my door). We walked on to my door, then we

near - ly lost my mind. Be - kissed a lit - tle more.
Whoa, _____ I

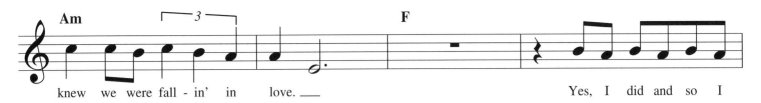

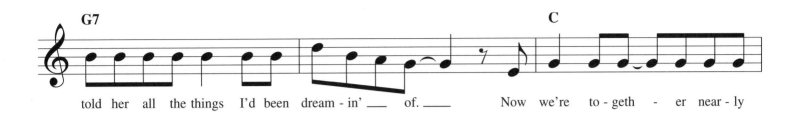

DOWN UNDER

Words and Music by COLIN HAY
and RON STRYKERT

Steady 4, with a Ska feel

Trav-el-ing in a fried-out com-bie

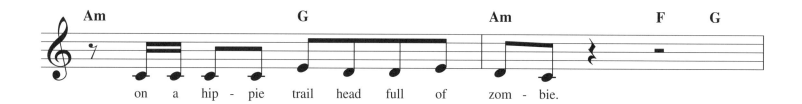

on a hip-pie trail head full of zom-bie.

I met a strange la-dy. ___ She made ___ me ner-vous.

She took me in ___ and gave me break-fast, and she said,

"Do you come from a land down un-der?" Where wom-en glow and men plun-

der? Can't you hear, can't you hear the thun-der? You

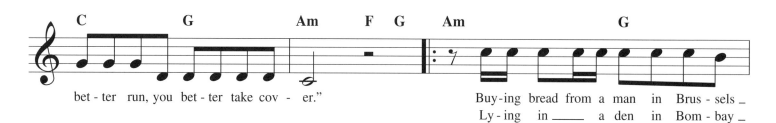

bet-ter run, you bet-ter take cov-er." Buy-ing bread from a man in Brus-sels ___
Ly-ing in ___ a den in Bom-bay ___

DRIFT AWAY

Words and Music by
MENTOR WILLIAMS

Moderately fast

Day af - ter day I'm more con -
Be - gin - ning to think that I'm wast - in'
And thanks for the joy that you've giv - en

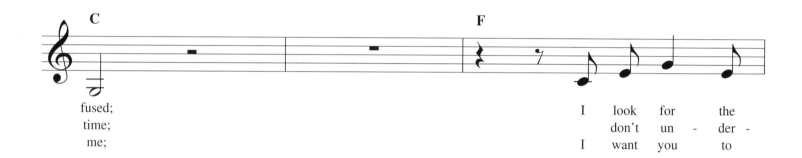

fused; I look for the
time; don't un - der -
me; I want you to

light in the pour - ing rain.
stand the things that I do.
know I be - lieve in your song,

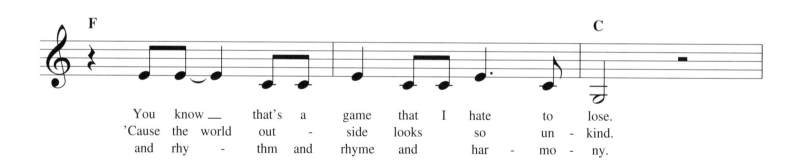

You know that's a game that I hate to lose.
'Cause the world out - side looks so un - kind.
and rhy - thm and rhyme and har - mo - ny.

I'm feel - in' the strain;
Now I'm count - in' on you
You help me a - long,

ain't __ it a shame? __
to car - ry me through. __
mak - in' me strong. __
Oh, give me the beat, __ boys, to

soothe my soul; __ I wan - na get lost in your rock __ and roll __ and

drift a - way. __ Give me the beat, __ boys, to

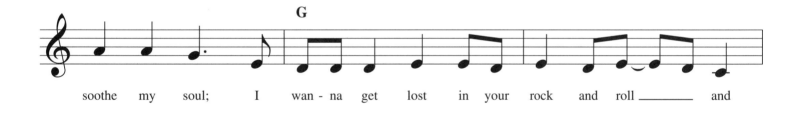

soothe my soul; I wan - na get lost in your rock and roll __ and

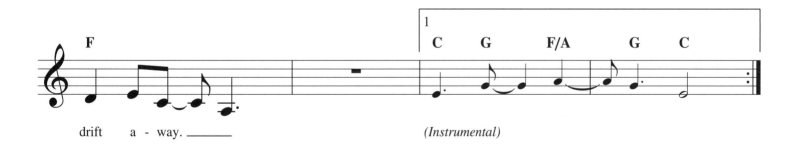

drift a - way. __ *(Instrumental)*

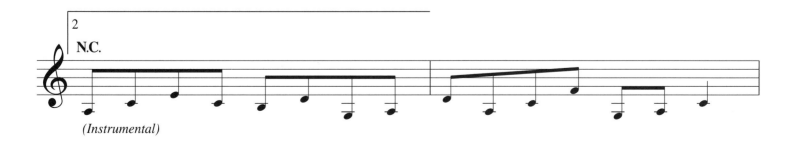

(Instrumental)

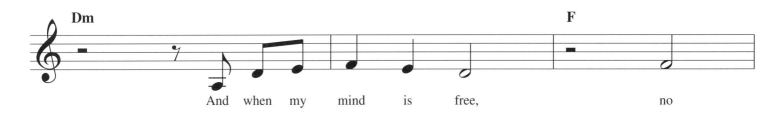

And when my mind is free, no

mel - o - dy ___ can move ___ me.

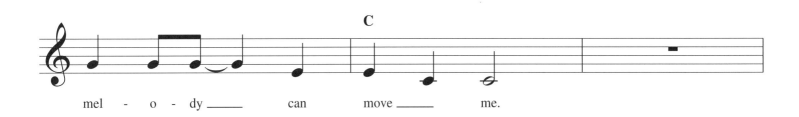

When I'm feel - in' blue, ___ gui - tars are

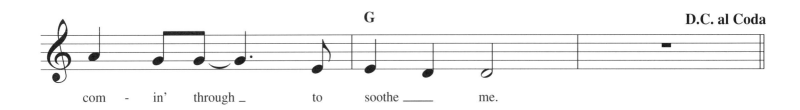

com - in' through _ to soothe ___ me.

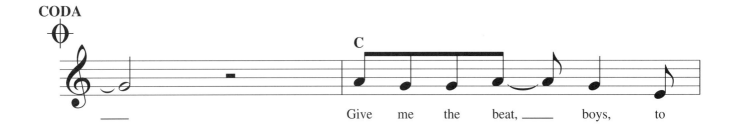

___ Give me the beat, ___ boys, to

soothe my soul; I wan - na get lost in your

rock and roll ___ and drift a - way. ___

EVERY ROSE HAS ITS THORN

Words and Music by BOBBY DALL,
C.C. DEVILLE, BRET MICHAELS
and RIKKI ROCKETT

Moderately

We both lie si-lent-ly still __ in the dead of the night. __ Al-though we
lis-ten to our fa-vor-ite song _____ play-ing on the ra-di-o, _____ hear the

both lie close to-geth - er _____ we feel miles a-part __ in-side. _____ Was it
D. J. say love's a game of eas-y come and eas - y go. ___ But I

some-thing I said or some-thing I did? Did my words not come out right? __ Though I
won - der does he know, _____ has he ev-er felt __ like this? And I

tried not to hurt you, __ though I tried. But I guess that's why __ they say,
know that you'd be here right now if I ____ could-'ve let you __ know some-how. __ I guess

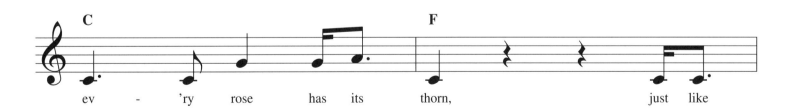

ev - 'ry rose has its thorn, just like

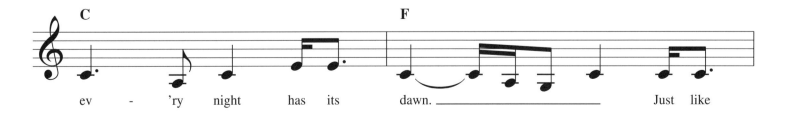

ev - 'ry night has its dawn. _____ Just like

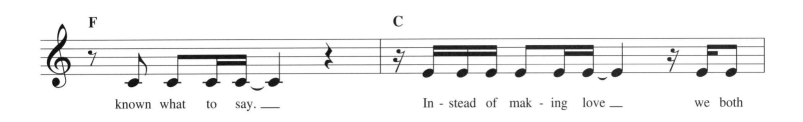

known what to say. ___ In - stead of mak - ing love ___ we both

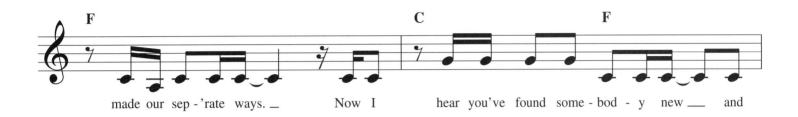

made our sep - 'rate ways. ___ Now I hear you've found some - bod - y new ___ and

that I nev - er meant that much to you. ___ To hear that tears me up in - side ___ and to

see you cuts me like a knife. I guess ev - 'ry rose has its

thorn, just like ev - 'ry night has its dawn. _____ Just like

ev - 'ry cow - boy _____ sings his sad, sad ___ song,

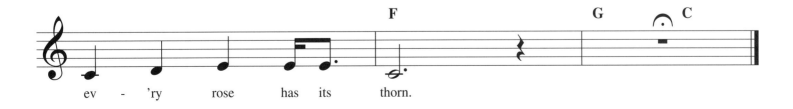

ev - 'ry rose has its thorn.

FIELDS OF GOLD

Music and Lyrics by
STING

FOREVER YOUNG

Words and Music by ROD STEWART,
KEVIN SAVIGAR, JIM CREGAN
and BOB DYLAN

Driving beat

May the good Lord be with you down ev-er-y road you roam. __

__ (Instrumental) And may

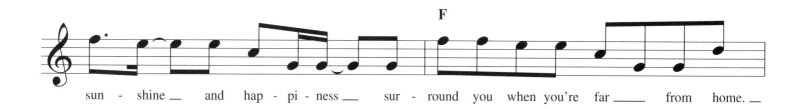

sun-shine __ and hap-pi-ness __ sur-round you when you're far ____ from home. __

__ (Instrumental) And may you

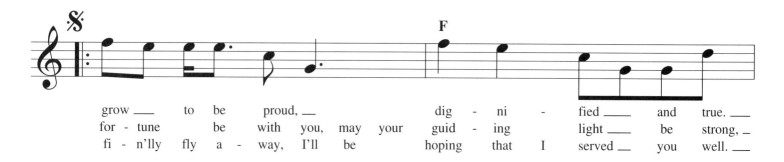

grow ___ to be proud, __ dig-ni-fied ____ and true. __
for-tune be with you, may your guid-ing light ____ be strong, __
fi-n'lly fly a-way, I'll be hoping that I served ___ you well. __

__ (Instrumental) And do un-to oth-ers as
build a stair-way to heav-en with a
For all the wis-dom of a life-time,

young. ___ (Instrumental)

And when you

For, for – ev – er young. _____ (Instrumental)

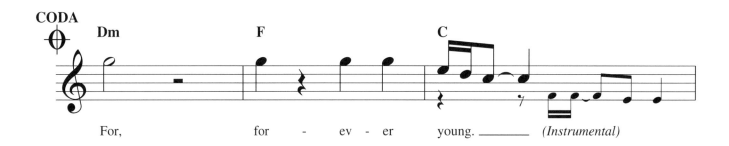

For – ev – er young. _____

FOREVER AND EVER, AMEN

Words and Music by PAUL OVERSTREET
and DON SCHLITZ

Lively Country

You   may think that   I'm_____ talk - in' fool - ish,   you've
time takes its toll_____ on a bod - y,   makes a

heard that I'm wild____ and I'm free.____   You may won-der how
young girl's__ brown__ hair__ turn gray.   Well, hon-ey, I don't care,__

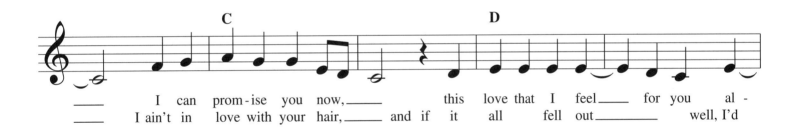

____ I can prom-ise you now,____   this love that I feel____ for you al -
____ I ain't in love with your hair,____ and if it all fell out_____ well, I'd

- ways will be.____   But you're not just time____ that I'm kill - in'.
love you an-y-way.____ They say   time can play tricks____ on a mem - 'ry,

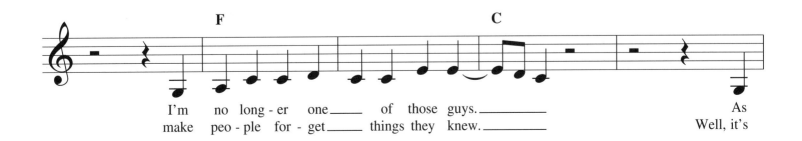

I'm no long-er one____ of those guys._____   As
make peo-ple for - get____ things they knew._____   Well, it's

sure as I live____ this love that I give_____ is gon - na be yours__
eas - y to see____ it's hap -'nin' to me._____ I've al - read - y for - got -

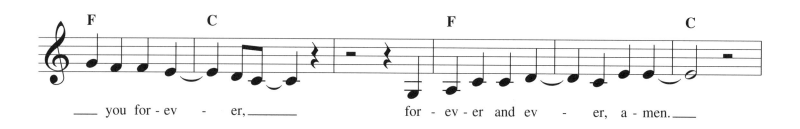

____ un - til the day that I___ die.____ Oh, ba - by, } I'm gon - na love__
- ten ev -'ry wom - an but__ you.____ Oh, dar - lin', }

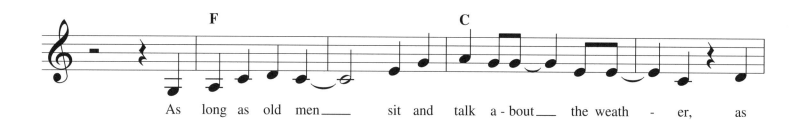

____ you for - ev - er,_____ for - ev - er and ev - er, a - men.___

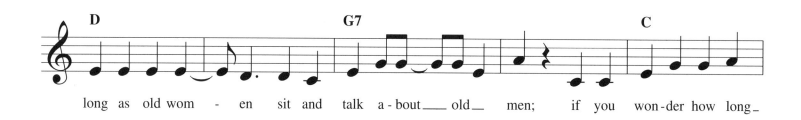

As long as old men____ sit and talk a - bout__ the weath - er, as

long as old wom - en sit and talk a - bout___ old__ men; if you won - der how long__

____ I'll be faith - ful, { I'll be hap - py to tell__
{ well, just lis - ten to how__

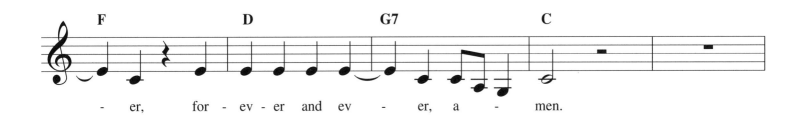

____ you a - gain.____
____ this song ends.

I'm gon - na love____ you for - ev - er and ev -

\- er, for - ev - er and ev - er, a - men.

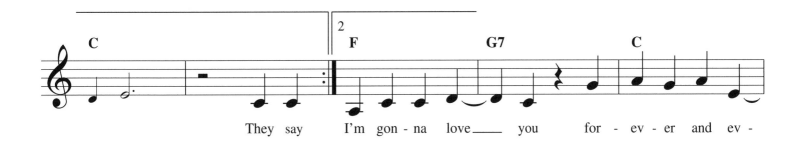

(Instrumental)

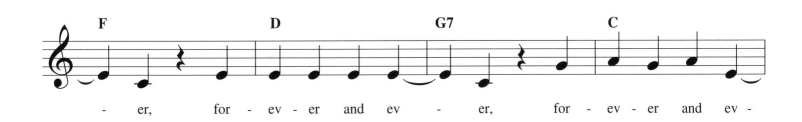

They say I'm gon - na love____ you for - ev - er and ev -

\- er, for - ev - er and ev - er, for - ev - er and ev -

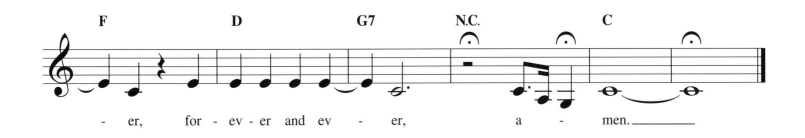

\- er, for - ev - er and ev - er, a - men.____

FREE RIDE

Words and Music by
DAN HARTMAN

With energy

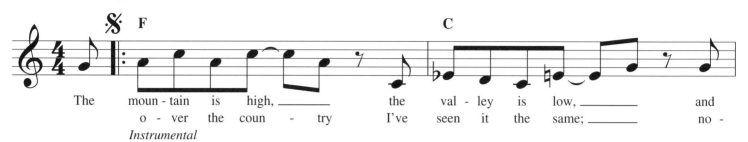

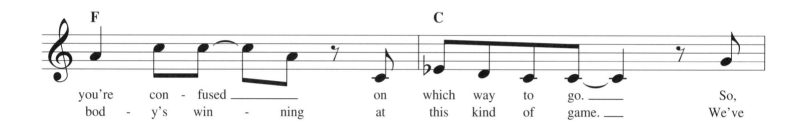

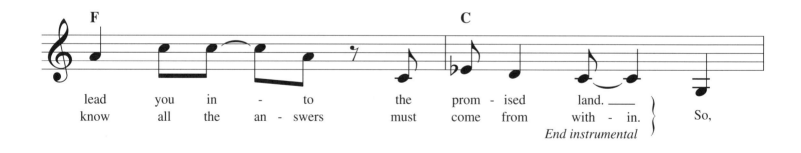

Come on _____ and sit here by my side. _____

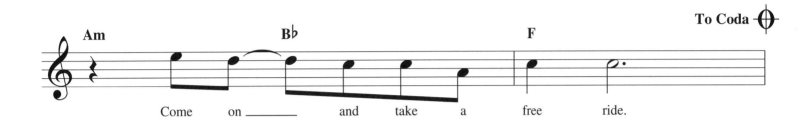

To Coda ⊕

Come on _____ and take a free ride.

(Instrumental)

D.S. al Coda

All Yeah, yeah, yeah, yeah.

CODA ⊕

Come on _____ and take a free ride. Yeah, yeah, yeah, yeah, yeah.

FUN, FUN, FUN

Words and Music by BRIAN WILSON
and MIKE LOVE

Bright Rock

Well, she got her dad-dy's car and she cruised through the ham-bur-ger stand ___
girls ___ can't ___ stand her 'cause she walks, looks and drives like an ace ___

___ now. ___ Seems she for-got all a-bout ___ the li-
___ now. ___ She makes the "In-dy" five hun - dred look

brar - y like she told her "old man" ___ now. ___ And with her
like a Ro-man char-i-ot race ___ now. ___ A lot-ta

ra - di - o blast - in', goes cruis-in' just as fast as she can ___ now. ___
guys try to catch ___ her, but she leads 'em on a wild ___ goose chase ___ now. ___

And she'll have fun, fun, fun, till her dad-dy takes the T - Bird a - way. ___

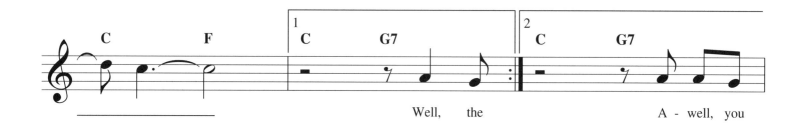

_____ Well, the A - well, you

knew all a - long ___ that your dad was get - tin' wise to you ___ now. ___

And since he took your set of keys, you've been think - in' that your fun is all through ___

___ now. ___ But you can come a - long with me, 'cause we

got a lot - ta things to do ___ now. ___ And you'll have

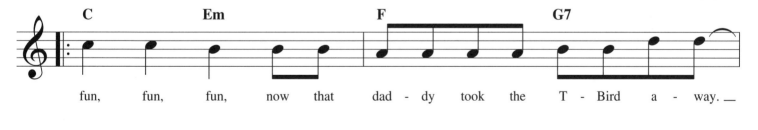

fun, fun, fun, now that dad - dy took the T - Bird a - way. ___

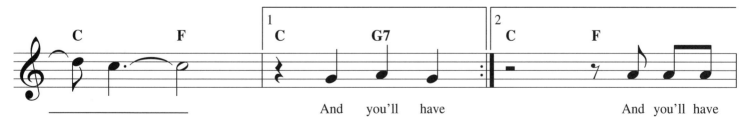

___ And you'll have And you'll have

fun, fun, fun, now that dad - dy took the T - Bird a - way. ___

GARDEN SONG

Words and Music by
DAVE MALLETT

Moderately

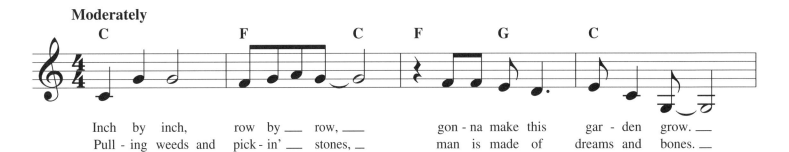

Inch by inch, row by row, gon-na make this gar-den grow.
Pull-ing weeds and pick-in' stones, man is made of dreams and bones.

All it takes is a rake and a hoe, and a piece of fer-tile ground.
Feel the need to grow my own 'cause the time is close at hand.

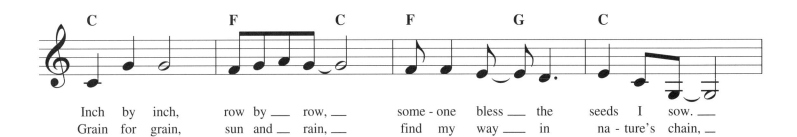

Inch by inch, row by row, some-one bless the seeds I sow.
Grain for grain, sun and rain, find my way in na-ture's chain,

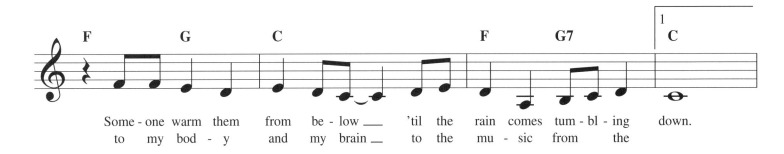

Some-one warm them from be-low 'til the rain comes tum-bl-ing down.
to my bod-y and my brain to the mu-sic from the

(Instrumental)
land.   (Instrumental)

GIRLS JUST WANT TO HAVE FUN

Words and Music by
ROBERT HAZARD

Bright Pop beat

I come home in the morn - ing light. ___ My moth-
The phone rings in the mid - dle of the night. My fa -
Some boys take a beau - ti - ful girl ___ and hide

- er says, "When ___ you gon - na live your life right?" ___
- ther yells, "What ___ you gon - na do with your life?" ___
___ her a - way ___ from ___ the rest of the world. ___

Oh, Moth - er dear, we're not the for - tu - nate ones. And
Oh, Dad - dy dear, you know you're still num - ber one. But
I want to be the one to walk in ___ the sun. Oh,

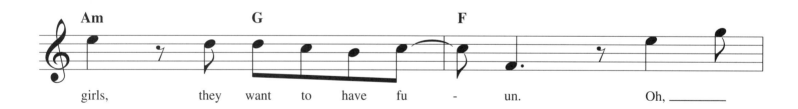

girls, they want to have fu - un. Oh, _____

girls just want to have fun. _____ *(Instrumental)*

girls just want to have...

That's all they real - ly want: _____

some fun. _____ When the work - ing day __

____ is done, ___ oh, girls, _____ they want to have fu -

un. Oh, _____ girls just want to have ___ fun. _____

D.C. al Coda
(take 2nd ending)

To Coda

(Instrumental)

CODA

They just wan - na they

just wan - na. _____ They just wan - na, they just wan - na. _____

Girls, _____ girls just want to have fu - un. _____

GO YOUR OWN WAY

Words and Music by
LINDSEY BUCKINGHAM

Moderate Rock

Lov - ing you   is - n't the right ____ thing ____ to do.
Tell ____ me why   ev - 'ry - thing turned ____ a - round.
Instrumental

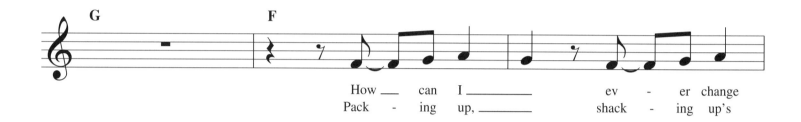

How ____ can I _____   ev - er change
Pack - ing up, _____   shack - ing up's

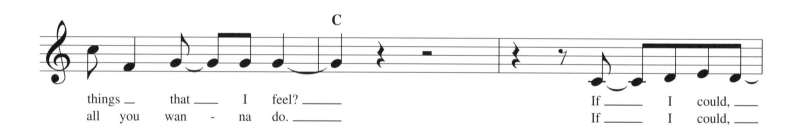

things __ that __ I feel? _____   If ____ I could, ____
all you wan - na do. _____   If ____ I could, ____

____   may - be I'd give ____ you __ my world. ____
____   ba - by, I'd give ____ you __ my world. ____

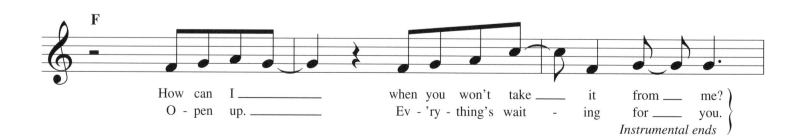

How can I _____   when you won't take ____ it from __ me?
O - pen up. _____   Ev - 'ry - thing's wait - ing for ____ you.
Instrumental ends

55

You can go _____ your own ___ way, _____

_____ go _____ your own ___ way. _____ You can call ___

___ it an - oth - er lone - ly day. _____

You can go _____ your own ___ way, _____ go ___

_____ your own ___ way. ___ your own ___ way.

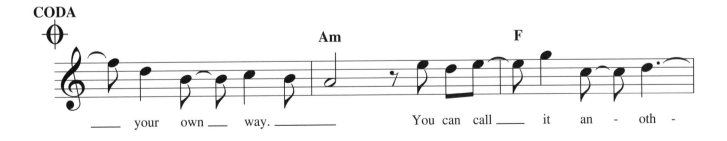

___ your own ___ way. _____ You can call ___ it an - oth -

- er lone - ly day. _____

GOOD RIDDANCE
(Time of Your Life)

Words by BILLIE JOE
Music by GREEN DAY

Fast

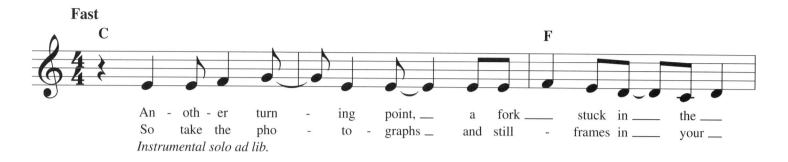

An - oth - er turn - ing point, __ a fork __ stuck in __ the __
So take the pho - to - graphs __ and still - frames in __ your __
Instrumental solo ad lib.

road.
mind.
Time grabs you by __ the __ wrist, __ di - rects __
Hang it on __ a __ shelf __ in good __

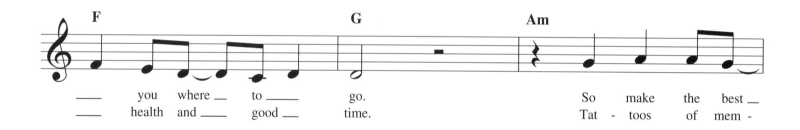

__ you where __ to __ go.
__ health and __ good __ time.
So make the best __
Tat - toos of mem -

__ of __ this test __ and don't __ ask why. _____
- o - ries and dead __ skin __ on trial. _____

It's not a ques - tion, but __ a les - son __ learned __ in __
For what it's worth, __ it __ was worth __ all __ the __

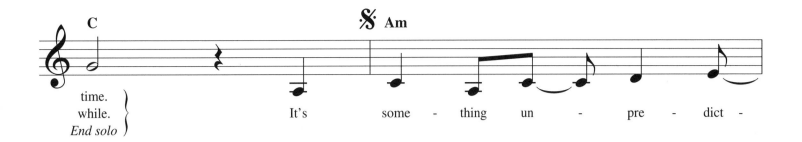

time.
while.
End solo

It's some - thing un - pre - dict -

- a - ble, _____ but in the end _____ it's right. _____

_____ I hope you had _____ the time _____

To Coda

_____ of _____ your life. _____

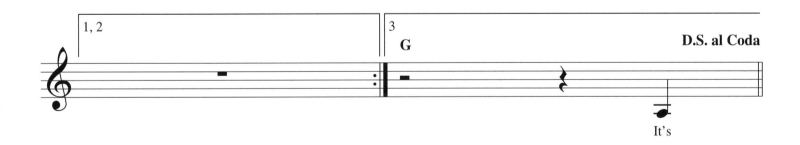

It's

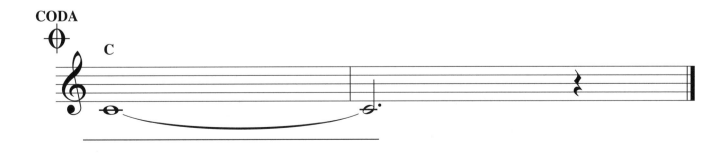

CODA

A GROOVY KIND OF LOVE

Words and Music by TONI WINE
and CAROLE BAYER SAGER

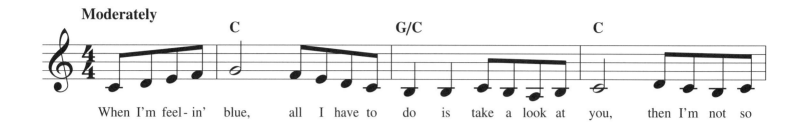

When I'm feel-in' blue, all I have to do is take a look at you, then I'm not so

blue. When you're close to me, I can feel your heart beat. I can hear you

breath - ing in my ear. Would - n't you a - gree, ba - by, you and

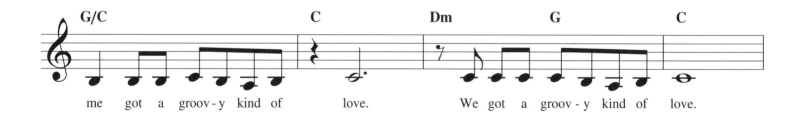

me got a groov-y kind of love. We got a groov-y kind of love.

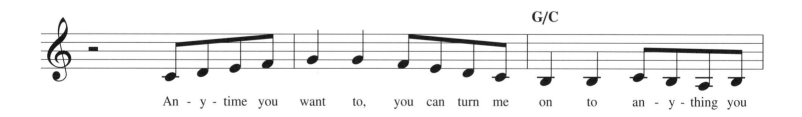

An - y - time you want to, you can turn me on to an - y - thing you

want to, an - y - time at all. When I taste your lips, oh, I start to

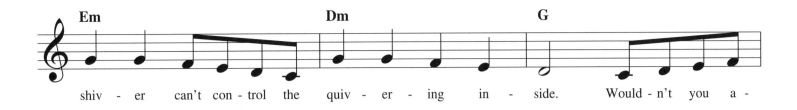

shiv - er can't con - trol the quiv - er - ing in - side. Would - n't you a -

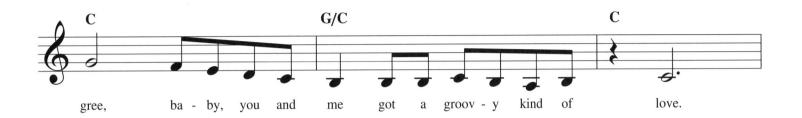

gree, ba - by, you and me got a groov - y kind of love.

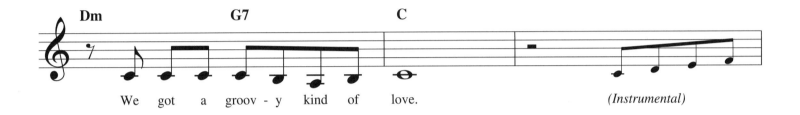

We got a groov - y kind of love. *(Instrumental)*

When I'm in your arms, noth - ing seems to mat - ter. If the world would

shat - ter, I don't care. Would - n't you a - gree, ba - by, you and

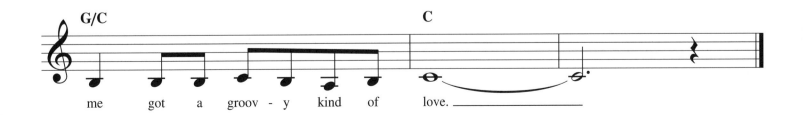

me got a groov - y kind of love. _____

HAVE YOU EVER SEEN THE RAIN?

Words and Music by
JOHN FOGERTY

HEY, GOOD LOOKIN'

Words and Music by
HANK WILLIAMS

Lively

Hey,   hey,   good   look - in',   what - cha got
free   and   read - y   in',   so   we _____ can go

cook - in'?   How's a - bout   cook - in'   some - thin' up ___ with
stead - y.   How's a - bout   sav - in'   all your time ___ for

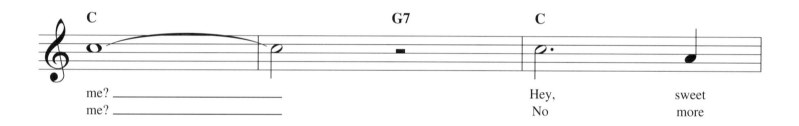

me? _____   Hey,   sweet
me? _____   No   more

ba - by,   don't ___ you think   may - be
look - in',   I   know ___ I've been   took - en.

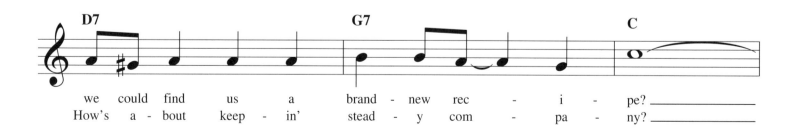

we could find   us   a   brand - new rec - i - pe? _____
How's a - bout keep - in'   stead - y com - pa - ny? _____

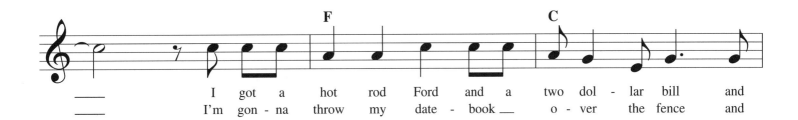

F **C**

I got a hot rod Ford and a two dol - lar bill and
I'm gon - na throw my date - book ___ o - ver the fence and

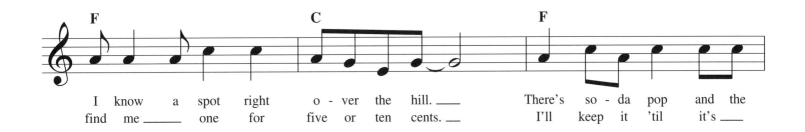

F **C** **F**

I know a spot right o - ver the hill. ___ There's so - da pop and the
find me ___ one for five or ten cents. ___ I'll keep it 'til it's ___

C **D7** **G7**

danc - in's ___ free, so if you wan - na have fun come a - long with me. ___
cov - ered with age ___ 'cause I'm writ - in' your name down on ev - 'ry page. ___

C

Hey, good look - in', what - cha got

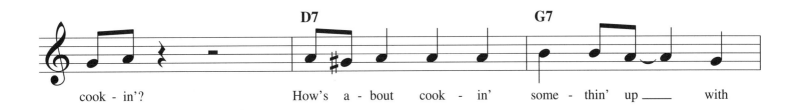

D7 **G7**

cook - in'? How's a - bout cook - in' some - thin' up ___ with

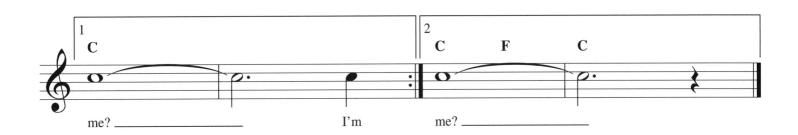

1
C

me? ___ I'm

2
C **F** **C**

me? ___

HEY, SOUL SISTER

Words and Music by PAT MONAHAN,
ESPEN LIND and AMUND BJORKLAND

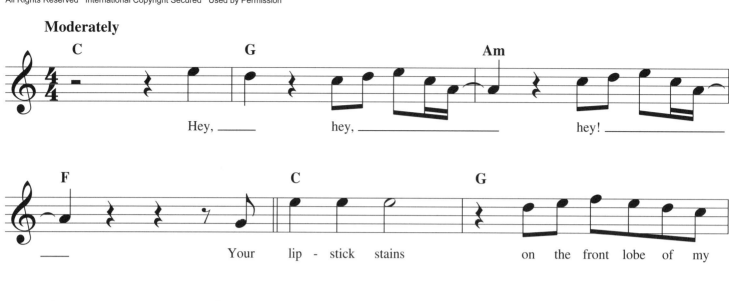

Hey, _____ hey, _____ hey! _____

_____ Your lip - stick stains on the front lobe of my

left - side brains. I knew __ I would - n't for - get ya, and so I went and

let you blow __ my mind. ____ Your

sweet moon - beam, the smell of you __ in ev - 'ry

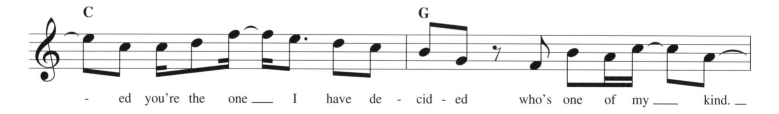

sin - gle dream I _____ dream, ____ I knew when we col - lid -

- ed you're the one __ I have de - cid - ed who's one of my __ kind. __

HOW TO SAVE A LIFE

Words and Music by JOSEPH KING
and ISAAC SLADE

Moderately

Step one, ____ you say, ____ "We need ____ to talk." ____ He walks, ____

____ you say, ____ "Sit down, ____ it's just ____ a talk."

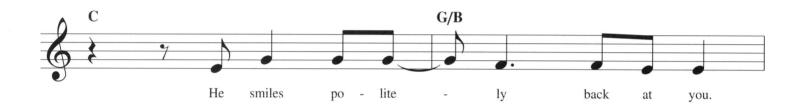

He smiles po - lite - ly back at you.

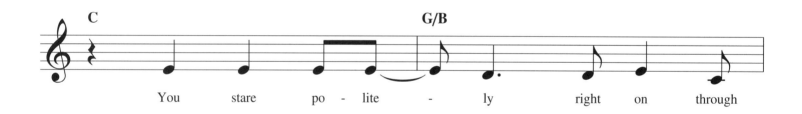

You stare po - lite - ly right on through

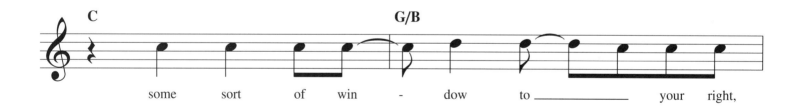

some sort of win - dow to ____ your right,

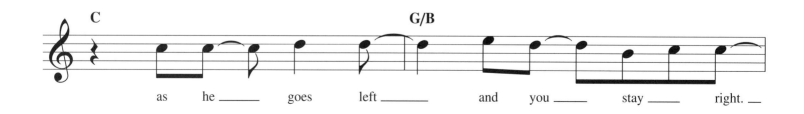

as he ____ goes left ____ and you ____ stay ____ right. ____

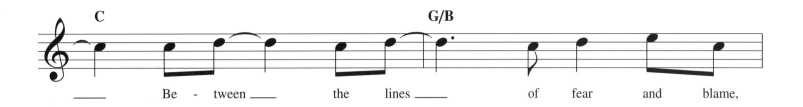

C   **G/B**

_____ Be - tween _____ the lines _____ of fear and blame,

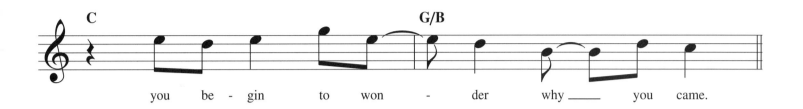

C   **G/B**

you be - gin to won - der why _____ you came.

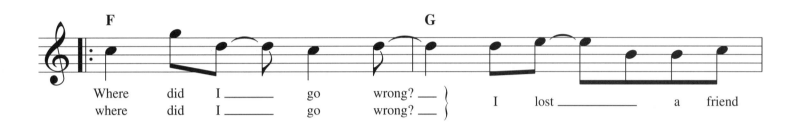

F   **G**

Where did I _____ go wrong? _____   I lost _____ a friend
where did I _____ go wrong? _____

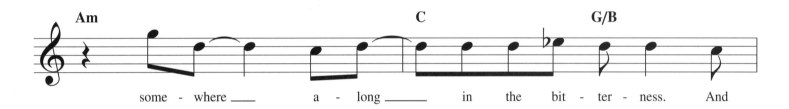

Am   **C**   **G/B**

some - where _____ a - long _____ in the bit - ter - ness. And

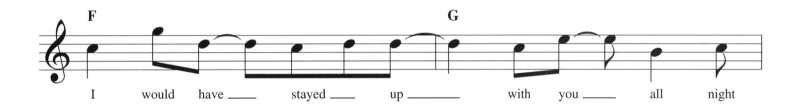

F   **G**

I would have _____ stayed _____ up _____ with you _____ all night

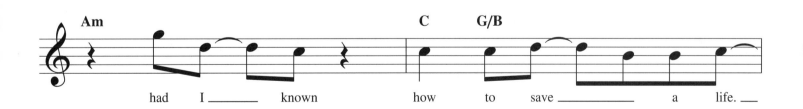

Am   **C**   **G/B**

had I _____ known how to save _____ a life. _____

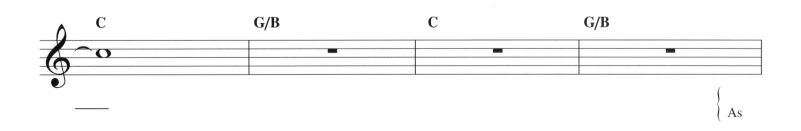

C   **G/B**   **C**   **G/B**

_____

{As

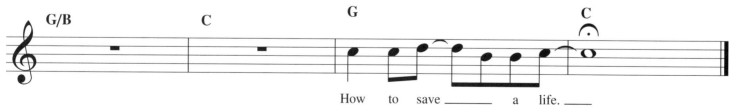

I'D LIKE TO TEACH THE WORLD TO SING

Words and Music by BILL BACKER,
ROQUEL DAVIS, ROGER COOK
and ROGER GREENAWAY

Additional Lyrics

2. I'd like to teach the world to sing in perfect harmony.
   I'd like to hold it in my arms and keep it company.

3. I'd like to see the world, for once, all standing hand in hand,
   And hear them echo through the hills for peace throughout the land.

I FEEL FINE

Words and Music by JOHN LENNON
and PAUL McCARTNEY

Bright Rock

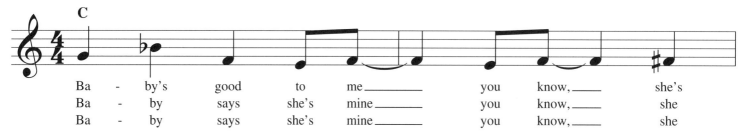

Ba - by's good to me you know, she's
Ba - by says she's mine you know, she
Ba - by says she's mine you know, she

hap - py as can be you know, she said so.
tells me all the time you know, she said so.
tells me all the time you know, she said so.

I'm in love with her and I feel fine.
I'm in love with her and I feel fine.
I'm in love with her and I feel fine.

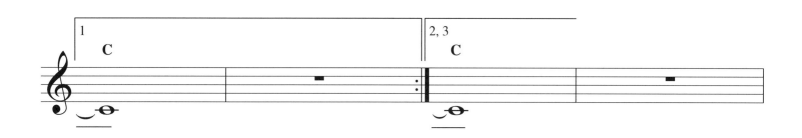

I'm so glad that she's my lit - tle girl,

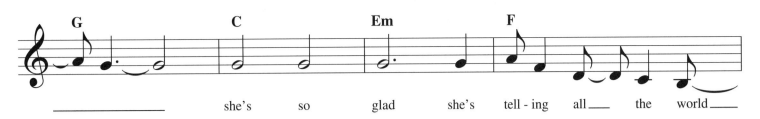

she's so glad she's tell-ing all the world

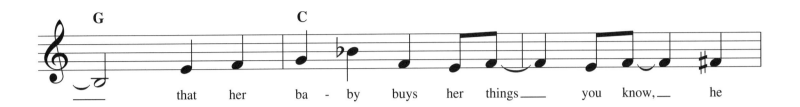

that her ba - by buys her things you know, he

buys her dia - mond rings you know, she said so.

F **To Coda**

She's in love with me and I feel fine.

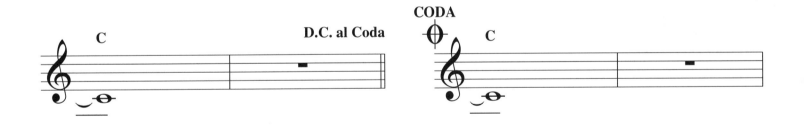

C **D.C. al Coda** **CODA** **C**

G **F** **C**

She's in love with me and I feel fine. *(Instrumental)*

I HEARD IT THROUGH THE GRAPEVINE

Words and Music by NORMAN J. WHITFIELD
amd BARRETT STRONG

Moderately

Mm. _____ I bet you're won-derin' how I knew 'bout your plans _____
2. _____ ain't sup-posed to cry, but these tears _____
3. *(See additional lyrics)*

_____ to make me blue, _____ with some oth - er guy _____ you knew be - fore.
I can't hold in - side. _____ Los - in' you _____ would end my life you see,

Be-tween the two of us guys _____ you know I loved you more. _____ It took me by sur -
'cause you mean _____ that much to me. _____ You could have told

prise _____ I must say _____ when I found out yes - ter - day. _____
_____ me your - self _____ that you loved _____ some - one else. _____

_____ Don't you know that I heard _____ it through the grape - vine, not much _____ long-
_____ In - stead I heard _____ it through the grape - vine, not much _____ long-

- er would you be _____ mine. Uh huh, heard it through the grape - vine.
- er would you be _____ mine. Oh, I heard _____ it through the grape - vine.

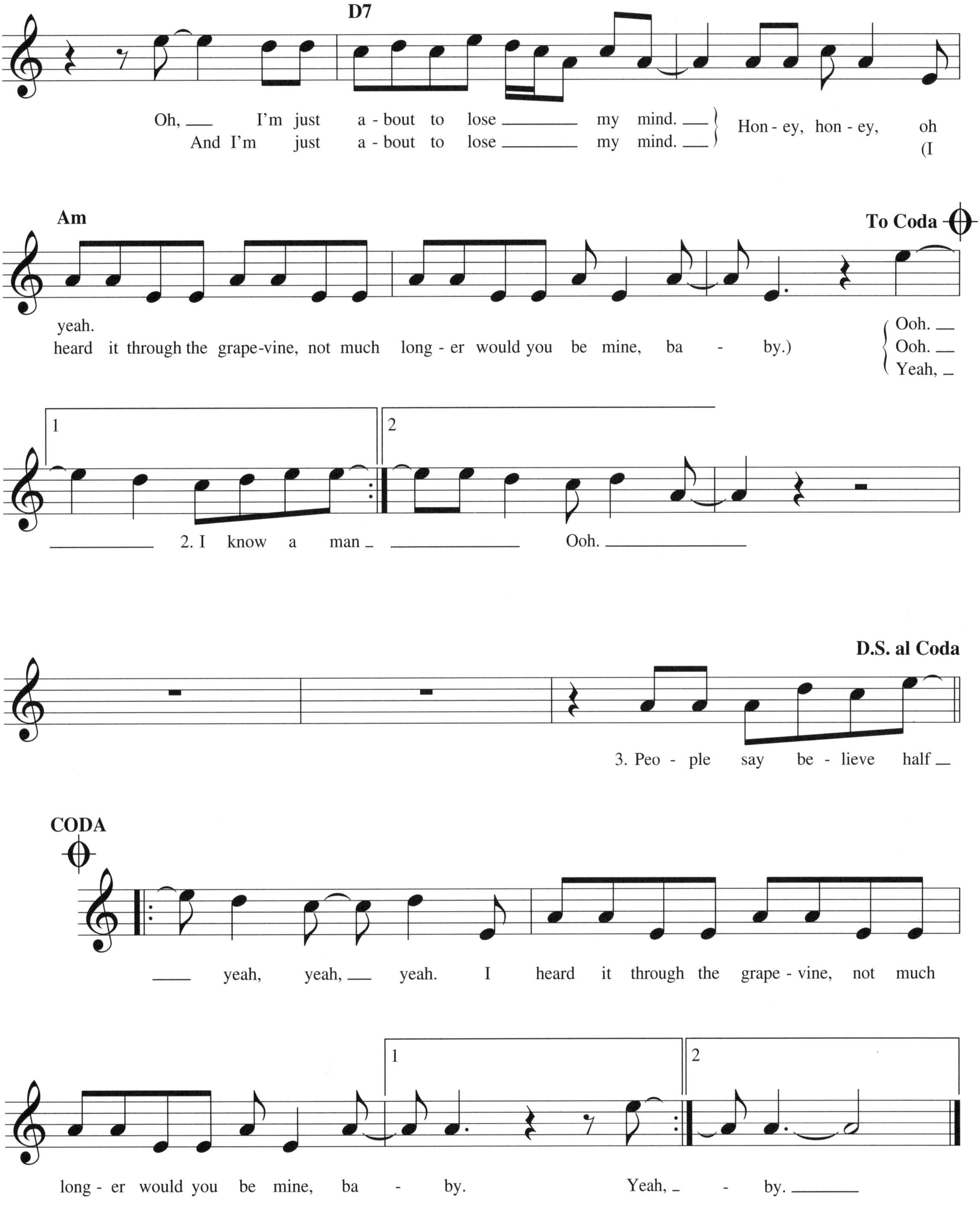
D7
Oh, I'm just a - bout to lose my mind.
And I'm just a - bout to lose my mind.
Hon - ey, hon - ey, oh
(I
Am
To Coda
yeah.
heard it through the grape-vine, not much long - er would you be mine, ba - by.)
Ooh.
Ooh.
Yeah,
1
2
2. I know a man
Ooh.
D.S. al Coda
3. Peo - ple say be - lieve half
CODA
yeah, yeah, yeah. I heard it through the grape - vine, not much
long - er would you be mine, ba - by.
Yeah, - by.

Additional Lyrics

3. People say believe half of what you see,
   Oh, and none of what you hear;
   But I can't help but be confused
   If it's true, please tell me, dear.
   Do you plan to let me go
   For the other guy you loved before?

I KNEW YOU WERE TROUBLE.

Words and Music by TAYLOR SWIFT,
SHELLBACK and MAX MARTIN

Moderately fast

Once up-on a time, a few mis-takes a-go,
No a-pol-o-gies, he'll nev-er see you cry. Pre-

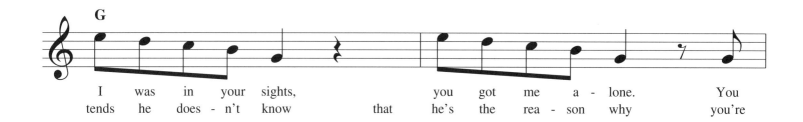

I was in your sights, you got me a-lone. You
tends he does-n't know that he's the rea-son why you're

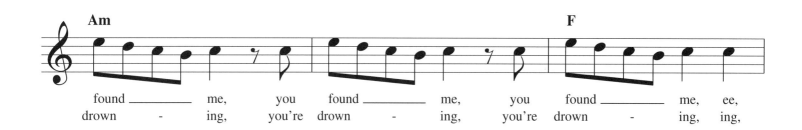

found _____ me, you found _____ me, you found _____ me, ee,
drown - ing, you're drown - ing, you're drown - ing, ing,

ee, ee, ee. I guess you did-n't care, and I guess I liked that. And
ing, ing, ing. And I heard you moved __ on, from __ whis-pers on the street. A

when I fell hard, you took a step back with - out _____ me, with-
new notch in your belt is all I'll ev-er be. And now _____ I see,

out _____ me, with - out _____ me, ee, ee, ee, ee. _____
now _____ I see, now _____ I see, ee, ee, ee, ee. _____

And he's long _____ gone when he's next _
He was long _____ gone when he met _

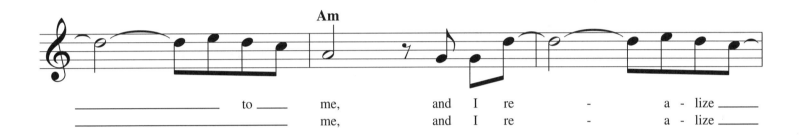

_____ to ___ me, and I re - a - lize _____
_____ me, and I re - a - lize _____

___ the blame is on ___ me. __ 'Cause } I knew you were
___ the joke is on ___ me. __

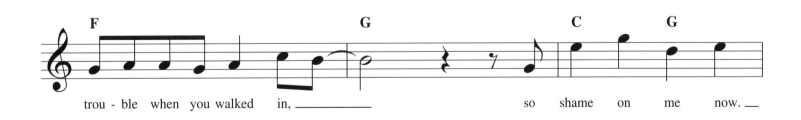

trou - ble when you walked in, _____ so shame on me now. __

___ Flew me to plac - es I'd nev - er been _____ till you

put me down. Oh, I knew you were trou - ble when you walked in, _____

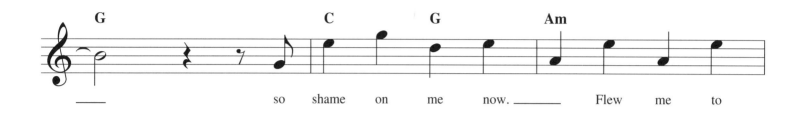

_____ so shame on me now. _____ Flew me to

plac - es I'd nev - er been. _____ Now I'm ly - ing on the cold, _ hard _

ground. Oh, _____ oh, _____ trou - ble,

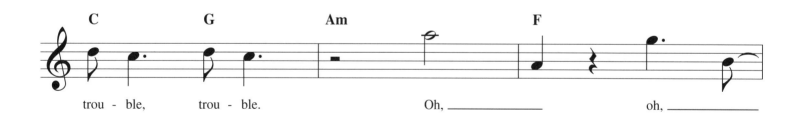

trou - ble, trou - ble. Oh, _____ oh, _____

_____ trou - ble, trou - ble, trou - ble. trou - ble, trou - ble. And the

sad - dest fear comes creep - ing in,

that you nev - er loved me or her, _____ or

D.S. al Coda

an - y - one or an - y - thing. Yeah, _____

CODA

trou - ble, trou - ble. I knew you were trou - ble when you walked in. _____

_____ Trou - ble, trou - ble, trou - ble. I knew you were

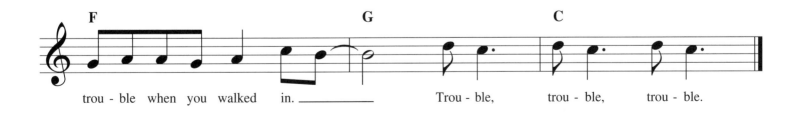

trou - ble when you walked in. _____ Trou - ble, trou - ble, trou - ble.

I LOVE HOW YOU LOVE ME

Words and Music by BARRY MANN
and LARRY KOLBER

Moderately slow

1. I love how you love ____ me. ____   I love how you kiss ____
2.,4. *(See additional lyrics)*
3. *(Instrumental solo)*

____ me; ____   and when I'm a - way ____ from you,

I love how you miss ____ me. ____   And I love the way ____

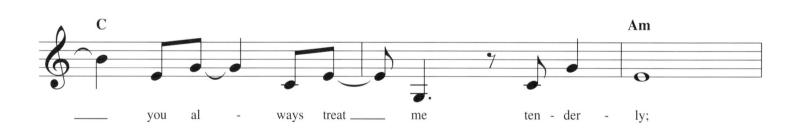

____ you al - ways treat ____ me ten - der - ly;

but, ____ dar - ling, most ____ of all,   I love how you love ____

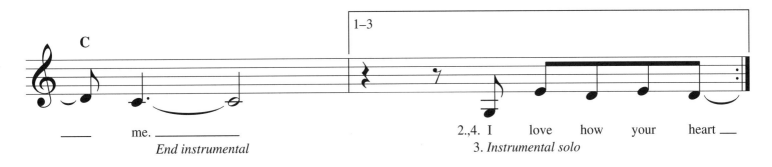

C   1–3

____ me. _____   2.,4. I   love   how   your   heart ___

End instrumental   3. *Instrumental solo*

4   **Am**

I   love   how   you   love _____ me. _____

F

I   love   how   you   love _____ me. _____

G   **C**

I   love   how   you   love ____ me. _____

Additional Lyrics

2.,4. I love how your heart beats whenever I hold you.
I love how you think of me without being told to.
And I love the way your touch is almost heavenly;
But, darling, most of all, I love how you love me.

I SHOT THE SHERIFF

Words and Music by
BOB MARLEY

Moderately slow, with a beat

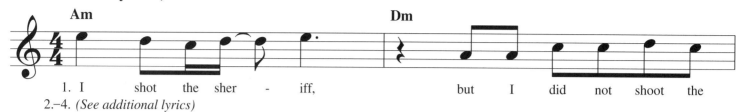

1. I shot the sher - iff, but I did not shoot the
2.–4. *(See additional lyrics)*

dep - u - ty. I shot the sher - iff,

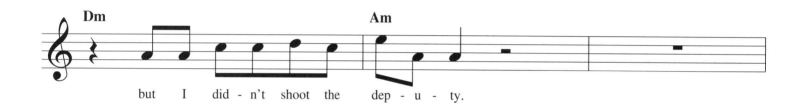

but I did - n't shoot the dep - u - ty.

All a - round in my home - town, they're try - ing to track me down.

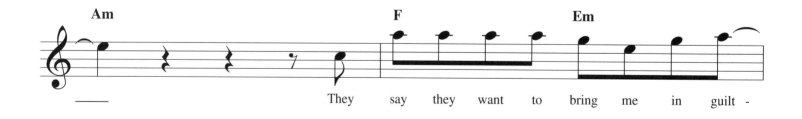

They say they want to bring me in guilt -

- y for the kill - ing of a dep - u -

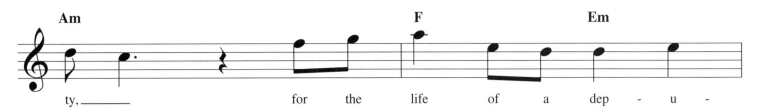

ty, _____ for the life of a dep - u -

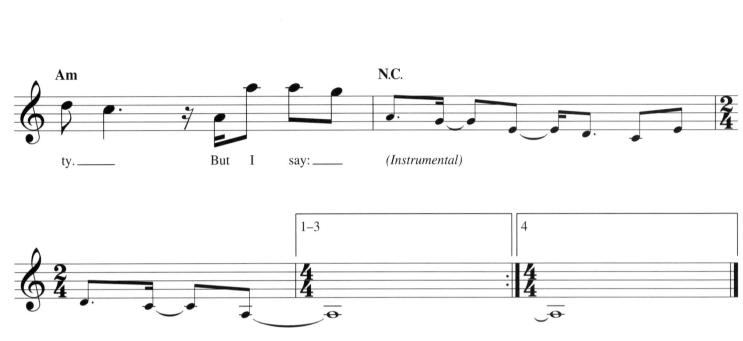

ty. _____ But I say: _____ *(Instrumental)*

Additional Lyrics

2. I shot the sheriff, but I swear it was in self-defense.
   I shot the sheriff, and they say it is a capital offense.
   Sheriff John Brown always hated me; for what, I don't know.
   Every time that I plant a seed, he said, "Kill it before it grows."
   He said, "Kill it before it grows." But I say:

3. I shot the sheriff, but I swear it was in self-defense.
   I shot the sheriff, but I swear it was in self-defense.
   Freedom came my way one day, and I started out of town.
   All of a sudden, I see Sheriff John Brown aiming to shoot me down.
   So I shot, I shot him down. But I say:

4. I shot the sheriff, but I did not shoot the deputy.
   I shot the sheriff, but I didn't shoot the deputy.
   Reflexes got the better of me, and what is to be must be.
   Every day, the bucket goes to the well, but one day the bottom will drop out.
   Yes, one day the bottom will drop out. But I say:

I'M A BELIEVER

Words and Music by
NEIL DIAMOND

I'VE JUST SEEN A FACE

Words and Music by JOHN LENNON
and PAUL McCARTNEY

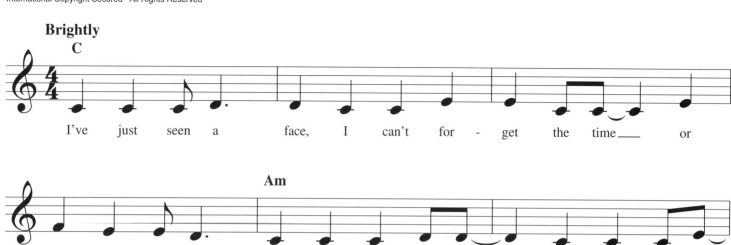

I've just seen a face, I can't for - get the time ___ or

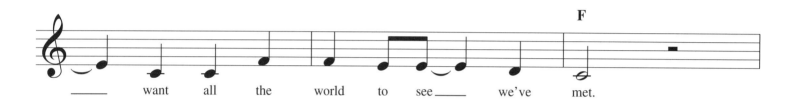

place where we just met. She's just the girl ___ for me, and I ___

want all the world to see ___ we've met.

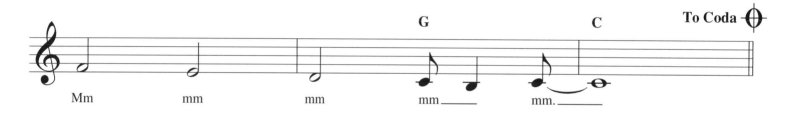

Mm   mm   mm   mm ___   mm.

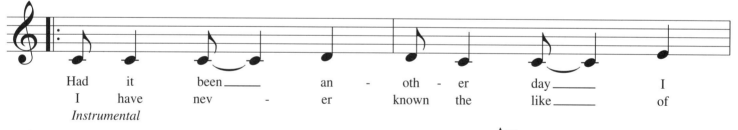

Had it been ___ an - oth - er day ___ I

I have nev - er known the like ___ of

might have looked the oth - er way ___ and I'd have nev - er been ___

this. I've been a - lone and I ___ have missed things and kept out ___

Instrumental

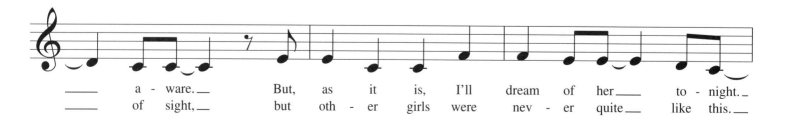

___ a - ware. But, as it is, I'll dream of her ___ to - night. ___

___ of sight, ___ but oth - er girls were nev - er quite ___ like this. ___

IF I HAD A HAMMER
(The Hammer Song)

Words and Music by LEE HAYS
and PETE SEEGER

Moderately

1. If I had a ham-mer, _____ I'd ham-mer in the morn-
2. bell, _____ I'd ring it in the morn-
3., 4. *(See additional lyrics)*

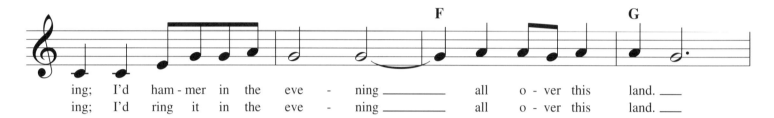

ing; I'd ham-mer in the eve - ning _____ all o - ver this land. __
ing; I'd ring it in the eve - ning _____ all o - ver this land. __

I'd ham-mer out dan - ger, __ I'd ham-mer out warn - ing, __
I'd ring __ out dan - ger, __ I'd ring __ out a warn - ing, __

I'd ham-mer out love be - tween my broth-ers and my sis - ters, }
I'd ring __ out love be - tween my broth-ers and my sis - ters, } all, ___

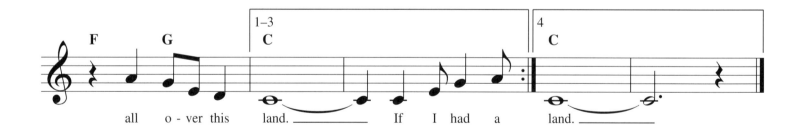

all o - ver this land. _____ If I had a land. _____

Additional Lyrics

3. If I had a song,
   I'd sing it in the morning;
   I'd sing it in the evening
     all over this land.
   I'd sing out danger,
   I'd sing out a warning,
   I'd sing out love between my
     brothers and my sisters,
   All, all over this land.

4. Well, I got a hammer,
   And I've got a bell,
   And I've got a song to sing
     all over this land.
   It's the hammer of justice,
   It's the bell of freedom,
   It's the song about love
     between my brothers and my sisters,
   All, all over this land.

IT'S A SMALL WORLD
from Disneyland Resort® and Magic Kingdom® Park

Words and Music by RICHARD M. SHERMAN
and ROBERT B. SHERMAN

Brightly

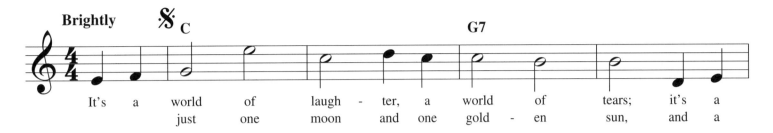

It's a world of laugh - ter, a world of tears; it's a
just one moon and one gold - en sun, and a

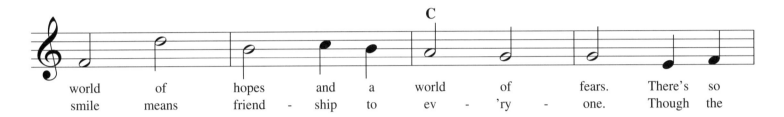

world of hopes and a world of fears. There's so
smile means friend - ship to ev - 'ry - one. Though the

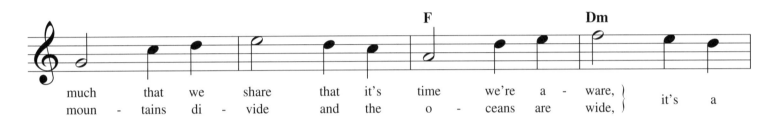

much that we share that it's time we're a - ware, it's a
moun - tains di - vide and the o - ceans are wide, it's a

small world af - ter all. _____ It's a small world

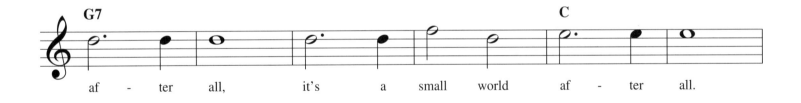

af - ter all, it's a small world af - ter all.

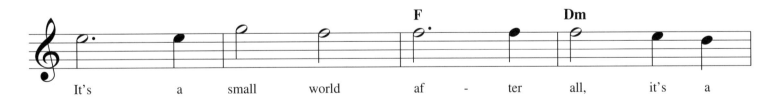

It's a small world af - ter all, it's a

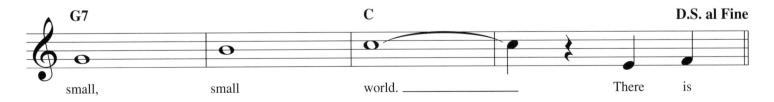

small, small world. _____ There is

IF I WERE A CARPENTER

Words and Music by
TIM HARDIN

Moderately

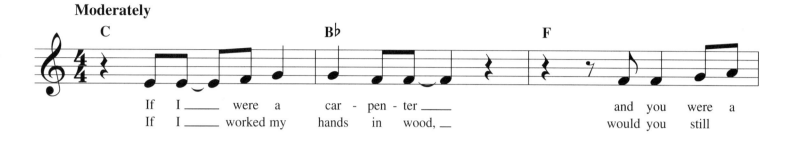

If I _____ were a   car - pen - ter _____   and you were a
If I _____ worked my   hands in wood, __   would you still

la - dy,   would you mar - ry me   an - y - way?
love me?   An - swer me,   babe, "Yes, I would,

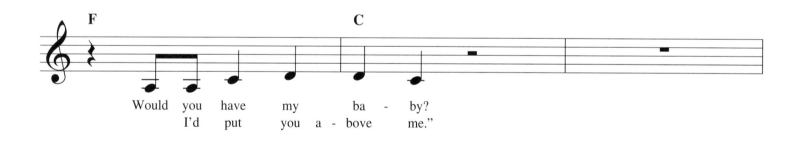

Would you have   my   ba - by?
I'd   put   you a - bove me."

If a tin - ker were a trade, __   would you still
If I were a mill - er,   at a mill wheel

love me?
grind - ing,
Car - ry - ing the pots I made, __
would you miss your col - ored box, __

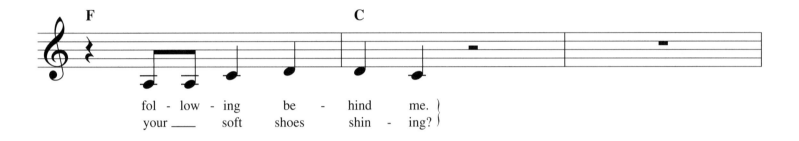

fol - low - ing be - hind me.
your __ soft shoes shin - ing?

Save my love through lone - li - ness, __ save my love for

sor - row. I've giv - en you my own - li - ness, __

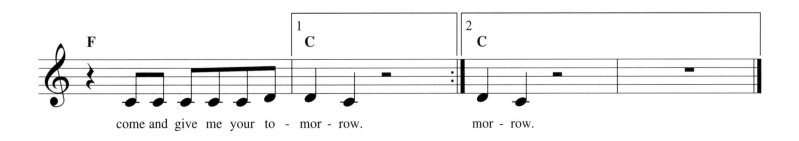

come and give me your to - mor - row. mor - row.

IT NEVER RAINS IN SOUTHERN CALIFORNIA

Words and Music by ALBERT HAMMOND
and MICHAEL HAZLEWOOD

Moderately

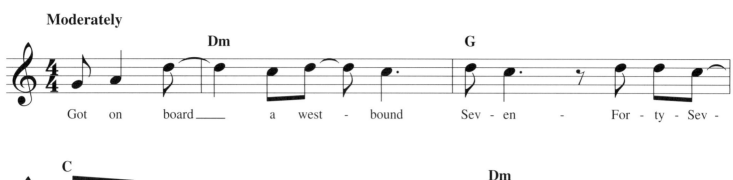

Got on board ___ a west - bound Sev - en - For - ty - Sev -

- en. ___ Did - n't think ___ be - fore ___ de - cid -

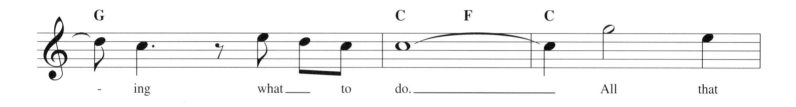

- ing what ___ to do. ___ All that

talk of op - por - tun - i - ties, T - V breaks ___ and mov -

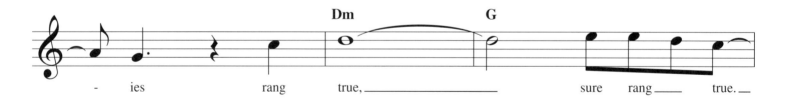

- ies rang true, ___ sure rang ___ true. ___

___ Seems it nev - er rains ___ in south -

- ern Cal - i - for - nia. ___ Seems I've of -

JESSIE'S GIRL

Words and Music by
RICK SPRINGFIELD

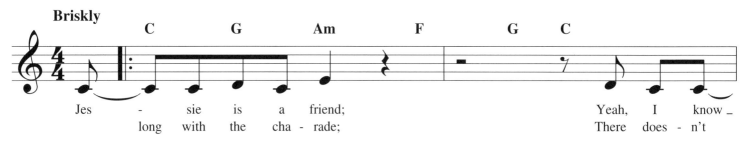

Briskly

Jes - sie is a friend; Yeah, I know _
long with the cha - rade; There does - n't

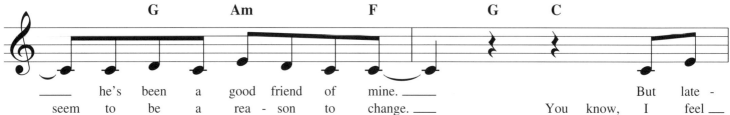

_____ he's been a good friend of mine. _____ But late -
seem to be a rea - son to change. ___ You know, I feel _

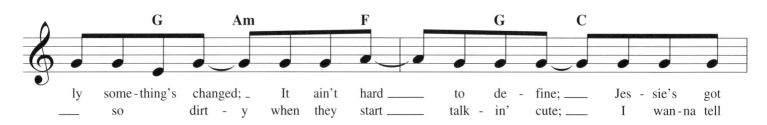

ly some-thing's changed; _ It ain't hard _____ to de - fine; ___ Jes - sie's got
___ so dirt - y when they start _____ talk - in' cute; ___ I wan-na tell

him - self a girl _____ and I wan - na make her mine. _____ And she's
her that I love _____ her, but the point is prob - 'ly moot. 'Cause she's

watch - in' him with those eyes, _____ and she's

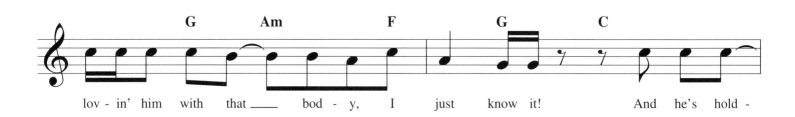

lov - in' him with that _____ bod - y, I just know it! And he's hold -

- in' her in his arms _____ late, late at night. _____

You know I wish that I had Jes - sie's girl, _____

I wish that I had Jes - sie's girl, _____

When can I find a _____ wom - an like that? I'll play a -

wom - an like that? Like Jes - sie's girl, _____ I wish that I had

Jes - sie's girl, _____ When can I find a _____

wom - an... When can I find a _____ wom - an like that?

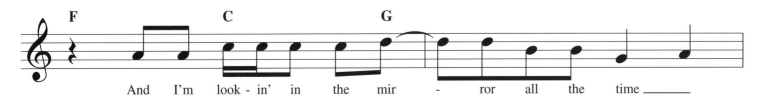

And I'm look - in' in the mir - ror all the time _____

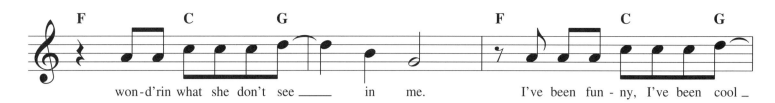

won-d'rin what she don't see _____ in me. I've been fun-ny, I've been cool _

_____ with the lines. _____ Ain't that the way love's sup - posed _

_____ to be? *(Instrumental)* You know I wish that I had

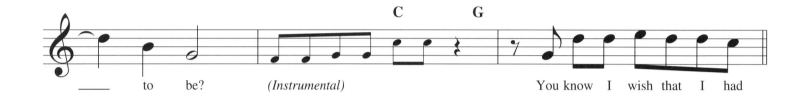

Jes - sie's girl, _____ I wish that I had

Jes - sie's girl, _____ I want Jes - sie's girl, _____

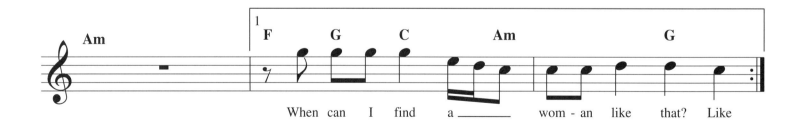

When can I find a _____ wom - an like that? Like

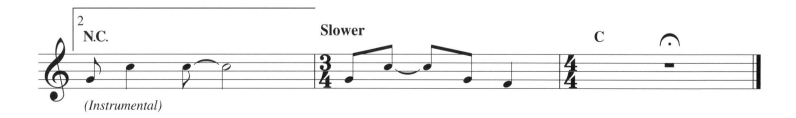

(Instrumental)

KISS THE GIRL
from Walt Disney's THE LITTLE MERMAID

Music by ALAN MENKEN
Lyrics by HOWARD ASHMAN

Moderate Calypso feel

There you see ___ her ___ sit - ting there a - cross the way. ___

___ She don't got a lot to say, ___ but there's some - thing a -

bout her. And you don't know why, ___ but you're

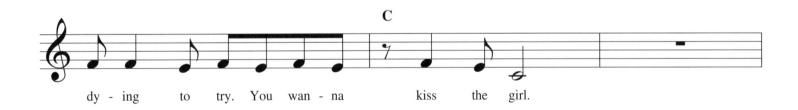

dy - ing to try. You wan - na kiss the girl.

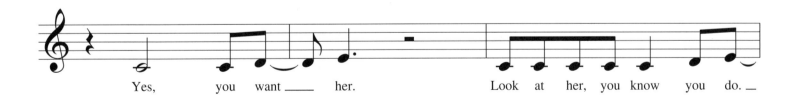

Yes, you want ___ her. Look at her, you know you do. ___

___ Pos - si - ble she wants you, too. ___ There is one ___ way to

ask her. It don't take a word, __ not a

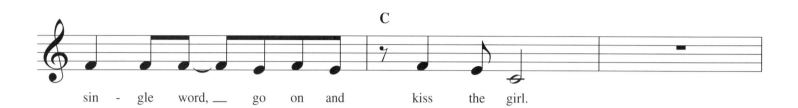

sin - gle word, __ go on and kiss the girl.

Sha la la la la la, my oh my. __ Look like the boy too shy. __ Ain't gon - na

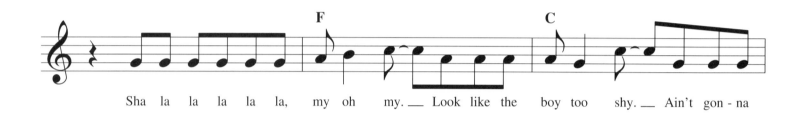

kiss the girl. Sha la la la la la, ain't that sad. __ Ain't it a

shame, too bad. __ He gon - na miss the girl. __ *(Instrumental)*

Now's your mo - ment, _____ float - ing in a blue la - goon. __

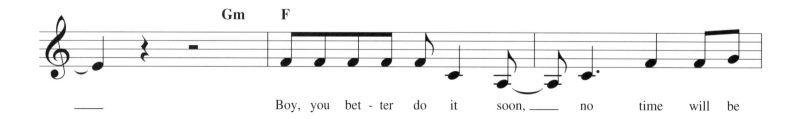

___ Boy, you bet - ter do it soon, ___ no time will be

bet - ter. ____ She don't say a word __ and she won't __

__ say a word un - til you kiss the girl. Sha la la la la la,
Sha la la la la la,

don't be scared. __ You got the mood pre - pared, __ go on and kill the girl.
float a - long __ and lis - ten to the song, __ the song say, "Kiss the girl."

Sha la la la la la, don't stop now. __ Don't try to hide it how __ you wan - na
Sha la la la la la, the mu - sic play. __ Do what the mu - sic say. __ You got - ta

kiss the girl. kiss the girl. You've _ got to kiss the girl.

You wan - na kiss the girl. You've got - ta kiss the girl.

Go on and kiss the girl. *(Instrumental)*

JIMMY MACK

Words and Music by BRIAN HOLLAND,
LAMONT DOZIER and EDWARD HOLLAND

Moderately

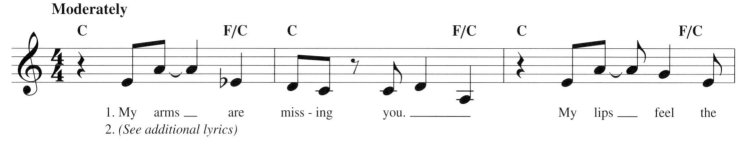

1. My arms __ are miss-ing you. __ My lips __ feel the
2. *(See additional lyrics)*

same way, too. __ I tried __ so hard to be true __

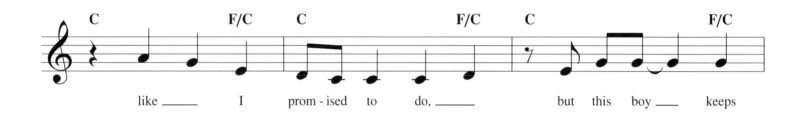

like __ I prom-ised to do, __ but this boy __ keeps

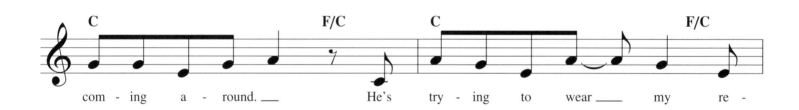

com-ing a-round. __ He's try-ing to wear __ my re-

sist-ance down. __ Hey, Jim-my, Jim-my, oh, __

Jim-my Mack, when are you com-ing back? Jim-my, Jim-

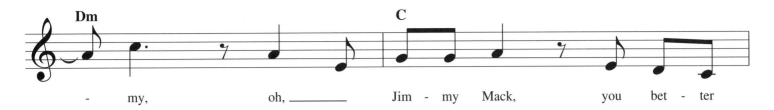

- my, oh, _____ Jim - my Mack, you bet - ter

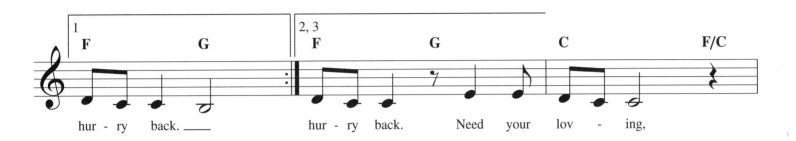

1
hur - ry back. ____

2, 3
hur - ry back. Need your lov - ing,

D.S. al Coda
(take 2nd ending)

To Coda

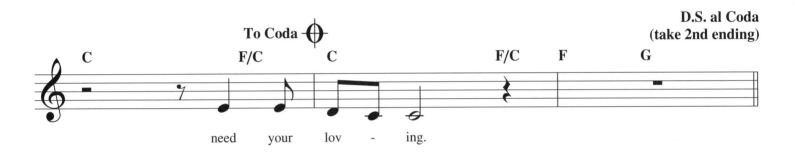

need your lov - ing.

CODA

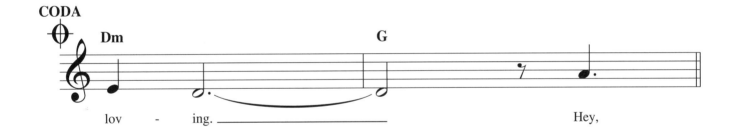

lov - ing. _____ Hey,

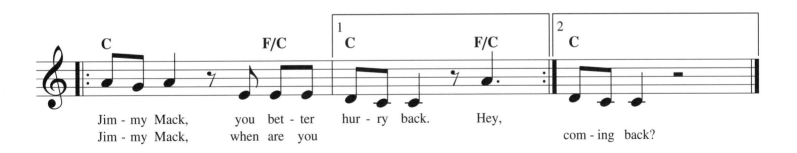

Jim - my Mack, you bet - ter hur - ry back. Hey,
Jim - my Mack, when are you

com - ing back?

Additional Lyrics

2. He calls me on the phone about three times a day.
   Now my heart's just listening to what he has to say.
   But this loneliness I have within keeps reaching out to be his friend.
   Hey, Jimmy, Jimmy, oh, Jimmy Mack,
   When are you coming back?
   Jimmy, Jimmy, oh, Jimmy Mack, you better hurry back.

KNOCK THREE TIMES

Words and Music by IRWIN LEVINE
and LARRY RUSSELL BROWN

Moderately

Hey, girl, what-cha do - in' down there   danc-in' a - lone ev - 'ry
you look out your win - dow to-night,   pull in the string with the

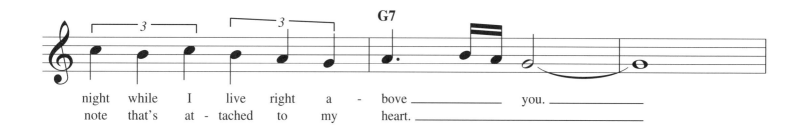

night while I live right a - bove _____ you. _____
note that's at - tached to my heart. _____

I can hear your mu - sic play - in', _____
Read how man - y times I saw _____ you, _____ how

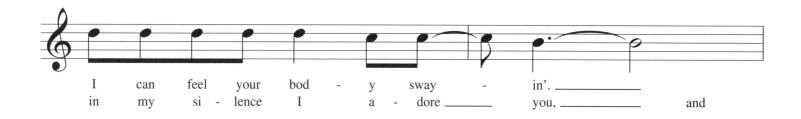

I can feel your bod - y sway - in'. _____
in my si - lence I a - dore _____ you, _____ and

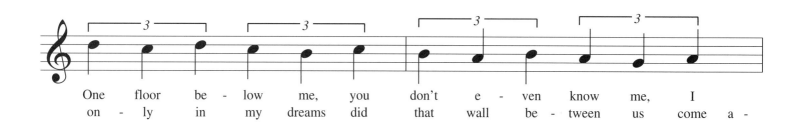

One floor be - low me, you don't e - ven know me, I
on - ly in my dreams did that wall be - tween us come a -

love _____ you.
part. _____

Oh, my dar - lin', knock three times on the ceil - ing if you

want ___ me; ___ twice on the pipe

if the an - swer is no. _____ Oh, my sweet - ness,

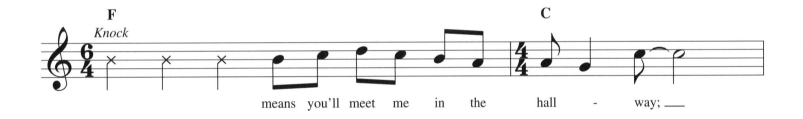

Knock

means you'll meet me in the hall - way; ___

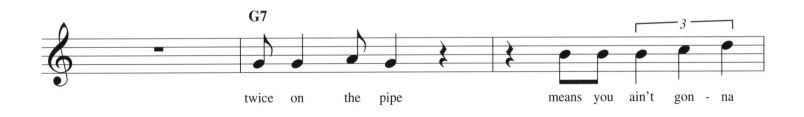

twice on the pipe means you ain't gon - na

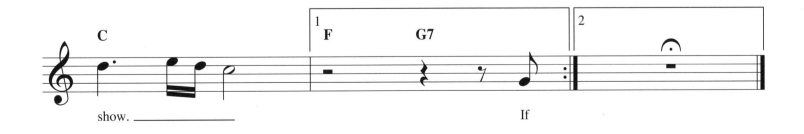

show. _____ If

KNOCKIN' ON HEAVEN'S DOOR

Words and Music by
BOB DYLAN

LAST KISS

Words and Music by
WAYNE COCHRAN

Moderately fast

Well, oh where, oh where can my ____ ba - by be? The Lord took her a -

way from me. ____ She's gone to heav - en so I got to be good ____ so

I can see my ba - by when I leave this world. ____

We were out on a date in my ____ dad - dy's car,
I woke up the rain was pour - ing down,

we had - n't driv - en ver - y far. ____ There in the road ____
there were peo - ple stand - in' all a - round. ____ Some - thing warm ____ was run - nin'

straight a - head ____ a car was stalled, the en - gine was dead. ____
in my eyes, ____ but I found ____ my ba - by some - how that night. ____ I

LEARNING TO FLY

Words and Music by TOM PETTY
and JEFF LYNNE

Moderate Rock

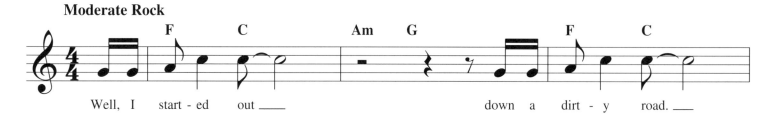

Well, I start - ed out _____ down a dirt - y road. _____

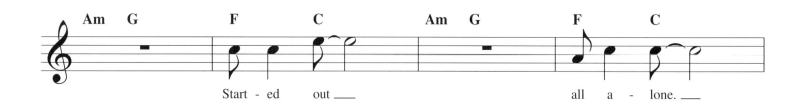

Start - ed out _____ all a - lone. _____

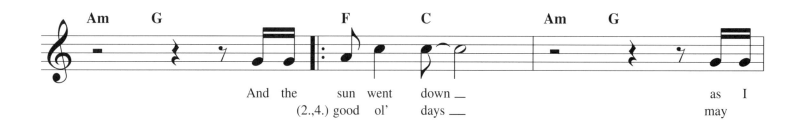

And the sun went down _____ as I
(2.,4.) good ol' days _____ may

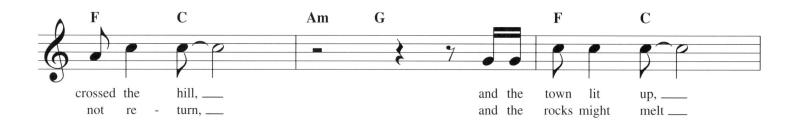

crossed the hill, _____ and the town lit up, _____
not re - turn, _____ and the rocks might melt _____

the world got still. _____ I'm
and the sea may burn. _____ I'm

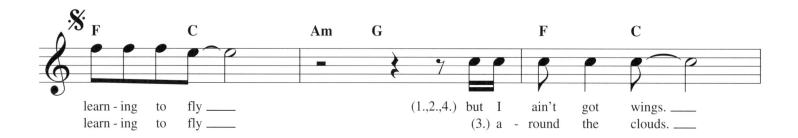

learn - ing to fly _____ (1.,2.,4.) but I ain't got wings. _____
learn - ing to fly _____ (3.) a - round the clouds. _____

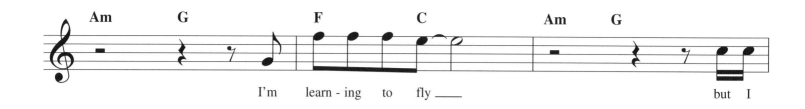

I'm learn - ing to fly ____ but I

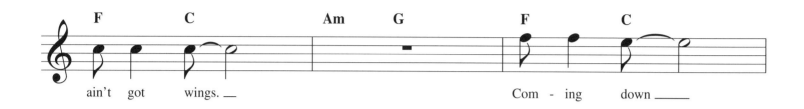

ain't got wings. ____ Com - ing down ____

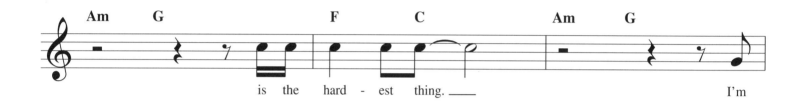

is the hard - est thing. ____ I'm

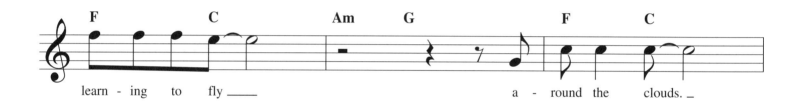

learn - ing to fly ____ a - round the clouds. ____

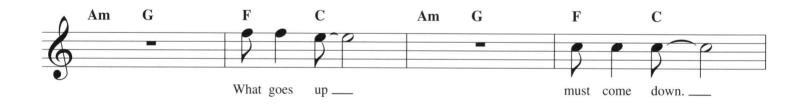

What goes up ____ must come down. ____

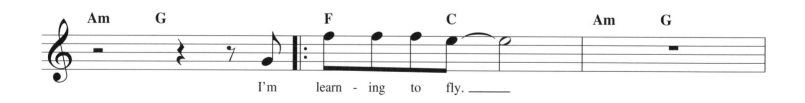

I'm learn - ing to fly. _____

I'm

LET'S GET TOGETHER
(Get Together)

Words and Music by
CHET POWERS

Moderately

Love is but the song we sing, and fear's the way we
Some will come and some will go, and we shall sure - ly
If you heard the song I sing, you must un - der -

die. _____
pass. _____
stand. _____

You can make the moun - tains ring, ___ or
When the one who left us here ___ re -
You hold ___ the ___ key to love ___ and

make the an - gels cry. _____
turns for us ___ at last, _____
fear all in your trem - bling hand. _____

Know the dove is
we are but a
One key ___ un -

on the wing, ___ and you need not ___ know why. _____
mo - ment's sun - light fad - ing on the grass. _____
locks them both you know and it's at your ___ com - mand. _____

Come on, peo - ple now, smile on your broth - er. Ev - 'ry - bod - y get to - geth - er, try and

To Coda   **1, 2**   **3**   **D.S. al Coda**

love one an - oth - er right ___ now. _____

CODA

Right ___ now! Right ___ now!

LET HER CRY

Words and Music by DARIUS CARLOS RUCKER,
EVERETT DEAN FELBER, MARK WILLIAM BRYAN
and JAMES GEORGE SONEFELD

Moderately slow Rock

She sits a - lone by a lamp - post _____

try'n to find a thought that's es - caped ___ her mind. _____

She says, "Dad's ___ the one I _____ love _____ the most, _____

but Stipe's ___ not far be - hind." _____

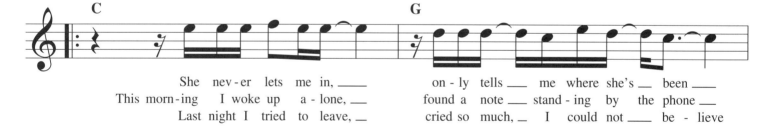

She nev - er lets me in, _____ on - ly tells ___ me where she's ___ been ___
This morn - ing I woke up a - lone, ___ found a note ___ stand - ing by the phone ___
Last night I tried to leave, ___ cried so much, ___ I could not ___ be - lieve

when she's had ___ too much to drink. _____
say - in', "May - be, may - be I'll be back some - day."
she was the same girl I fell in love with long a - go.

I say that I don't ___ care, ___ I just run my hands through her dark hair, ___ and I
I want - ed to look for you; ___ you walked in. I did - n't know just what to do, ___ so I
She went in the back ___ to ___ get high. I sat down on my couch and cried, ___ yell - ing,

LITTLE SISTER

Words and Music by DOC POMUS
and MORT SHUMAN

Brightly

(Instrumental)   Lit - tle sis - ter, don't you,

(Instrumental)   lit - tle sis - ter, don't you,

(Instrumental)   lit - tle sis - ter, don't you

kiss me once or twice, tell _____ me that it's nice and then you

run. _____ Yeah, yeah, _____

_____ lit - tle sis - ter, don't you do what your big sis - ter

MASSACHUSETTS
(The Lights Went Out)

Words and Music by BARRY GIBB,
ROBIN GIBB and MAURICE GIBB

Moderately

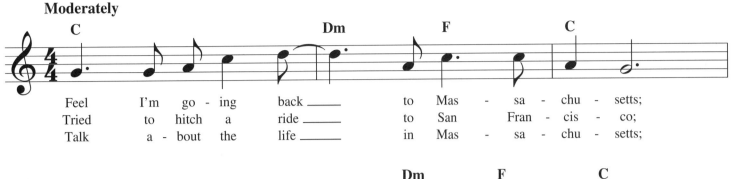

Feel   I'm   go - ing   back ____   to Mas - sa - chu - setts;
Tried   to   hitch   a   ride ____   to San   Fran - cis - co;
Talk   a - bout   the   life ____   in Mas - sa - chu - setts;

some - thing's tell - ing   me ____   I   must   go   home. __
got - ta   do   the   things __   I   wan - na   do. ____
speak   a - bout   the   peo - ple   I   have   seen. __

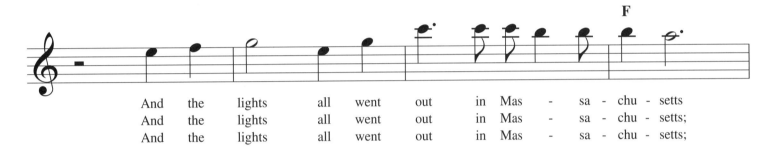

And   the   lights   all   went   out   in Mas - sa - chu - setts
And   the   lights   all   went   out   in Mas - sa - chu - setts;
And   the   lights   all   went   out   in Mas - sa - chu - setts;

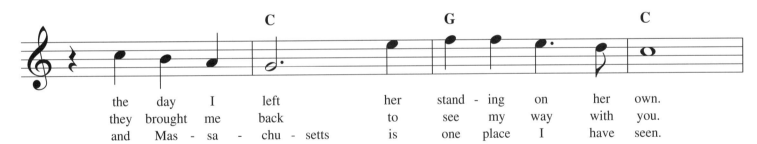

the   day   I   left   her   stand - ing   on   her   own.
they   brought   me   left   back   to   see   my   way   with   you.
and   Mas - sa - chu - setts   is   one   place   I   have   seen.

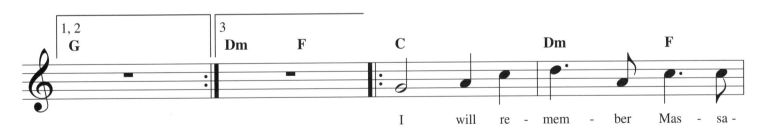

I   will   re - mem - ber   Mas - sa -

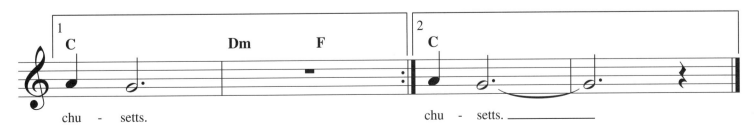

chu - setts.   chu - setts. ____

LOOKIN' OUT MY BACK DOOR

Words and Music by
JOHN FOGERTY

Moderately fast

Just got home from Il - li - nois, _____
gi - ant do - ing cart - wheels, a
For - ward trou - bles Il - li - nois, _____

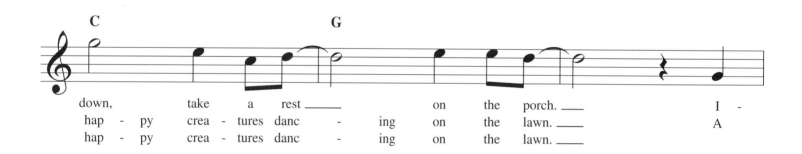

lock the front _____ door, oh boy! Got to _____ sit
stat - ue wear - in' high heels. Look at all the
lock the front _____ door, oh boy! Look at all the

down, take a rest _____ on the porch. _____ I -
hap - py crea - tures danc - ing on the lawn. _____ A
hap - py crea - tures danc - ing on the lawn. _____

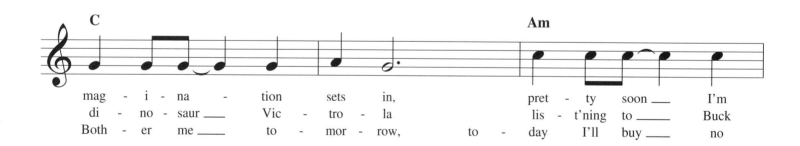

mag - i - na - tion sets in, pret - ty soon _____ I'm
di - no - saur _____ Vic - tro - la lis - t'ning to _____ Buck
Both - er me _____ to - mor - row, to - day I'll buy _____ no

To Coda ⊕

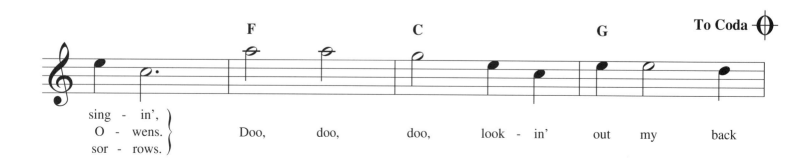

sing - in',
O - wens. } Doo, doo, doo, look - in' out my back
sor - rows.

LOVE STINKS

Words and Music by PETER WOLF
and SETH JUSTMAN

Moderately

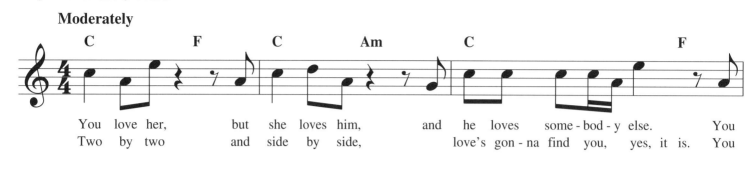

You love her, but she loves him, and he loves some-bod-y else. You
Two by two and side by side, love's gon-na find you, yes, it is. You

just can't win. And so ___ it goes 'til the day you die. ___ This
just can't hide. You'll feel ___ it call, your heart will fall, ___ then

thing they call love, ___ it's gon-na make you cry. ___ I've had the blues, the
love ___ will fly. ___ It's gone; that's all. ___ I don't care what an - y

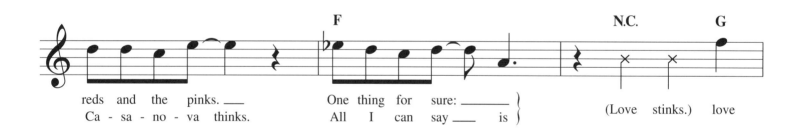

reds and the pinks. ___ One thing for sure: _____ (Love stinks.) love
Ca - sa - no - va thinks. All I can say ___ is

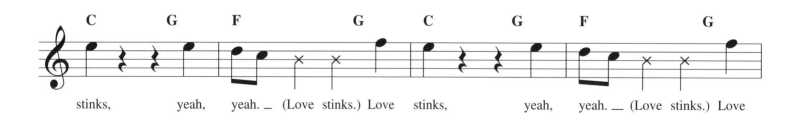

stinks, yeah, yeah. __ (Love stinks.) Love stinks, yeah, yeah. __ (Love stinks.) Love

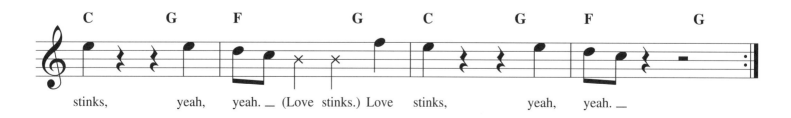

stinks, yeah, yeah. __ (Love stinks.) Love stinks, yeah, yeah. __

MEMORIES ARE MADE OF THIS

Words and Music by RICHARD DEHR,
FRANK MILLER and TERRY GILKYSON

Take one fresh and ten - der kiss, ____
Don't for - get a small moon - beam, ____

add one stol - en night of bliss. ____
fold in light - ly with a dream. ____

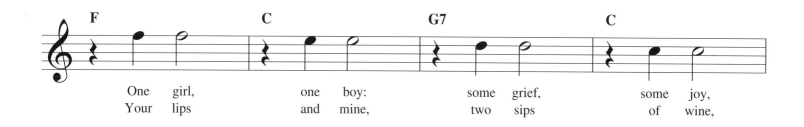

One girl, one boy: some grief, some joy,
Your lips and mine, two sips of wine,

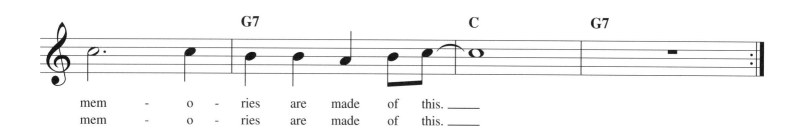

mem - o - ries are made of this. ____
mem - o - ries are made of this. ____

Then add the wed - ding bells, ___ one house where lov - ers dwell, ___

three lit - tle kids for the fla - vor. ____

Stir care - f'lly thru the days; __ see how the fla - vor stays. __

These are the dreams you will sa - vor.

With His bless - ings from a - bove, ____

serve it gen - 'rous - ly with love. ____

One man, one wife: one love thru life,

mem - o - ries are made of this. ____

MR. TAMBOURINE MAN

Words and Music by
BOB DYLAN

Moderately

Hey! Mis - ter Tam - bou - rine Man, play a song for me, I'm not

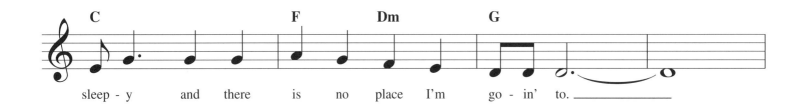

sleep - y and there is no place I'm go - in' to. _____

Hey! Mis - ter Tam - bou - rine Man, play a song for me, in the

To Coda ⊕

jin - gle jan - gle morn - in' I'll come fol - low - in' you. _____

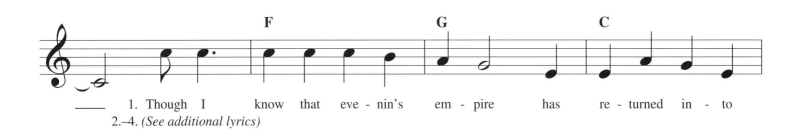

_____ 1. Though I know that eve - nin's em - pire has re - turned in - to

2.–4. *(See additional lyrics)*

sand, van - ished from my hand, left me blind - ly here to

stand but still not sleep-in'! _____ My wea-ri-ness a-

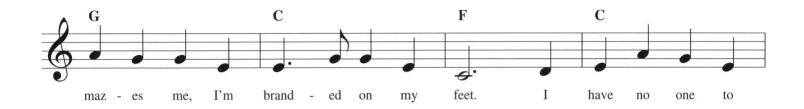

maz-es me, I'm brand-ed on my feet. I have no one to

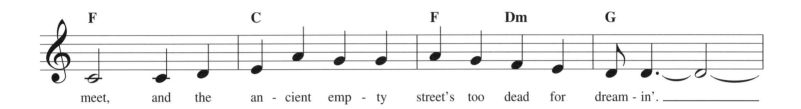

meet, and the an-cient emp-ty street's too dead for dream-in'. _____

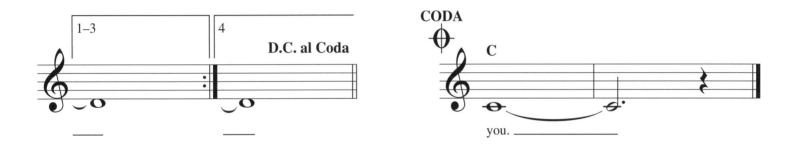

you. _____

Additional Lyrics

2. Take me on a trip upon your magic swirlin' ship
   My senses have been stripped, my hands can't feel to grip
   My toes too numb to step, wait only for my boot heels
   To be wanderin'
   I'm ready to go anywhere, I'm ready for to fade
   Into my own parade, cast your dancin' spell my way
   I promise to go under it.

3. Though you might hear laughin' spinnin' swingin' madly across the sun
   It's not aimed at anyone, it's just escapin' on the run
   And but for the sky there are no fences facin'
   And if you hear vague traces of skippin' reels of rhyme
   To your tambourine in time, it's just a ragged clown behind
   I wouldn't pay it any mind, it's just a shadow you're
   Seein' that he's chasin'.

4. Then take me disappearin' through the smoke rings of my mind
   Down the foggy ruins of time, far past the frozen leaves
   The haunted, frightened trees out to the windy beach
   Far from the twisted reach of crazy sorrow
   Yes, to dance beneath the diamond sky with one hand wavin' free
   Silhouetted by the sea, circled by the circus sands
   With all memory and fate driven deep beneath the waves
   Let me forget about today until tomorrow.

THE NIGHT THEY DROVE OLD DIXIE DOWN

Words and Music by
ROBBIE ROBERTSON

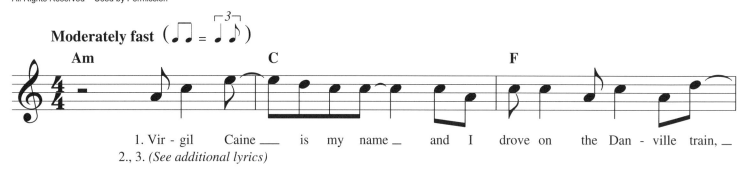

1. Vir - gil   Caine ___   is   my   name ___   and   I   drove   on   the   Dan - ville   train, ___
2., 3. *(See additional lyrics)*

_____   'til   Stone - man's   cav - al - ry   came ___   and

tore   up   the   tracks   a - gain. _____   In   the   win - ter   of   six -

ty - five,   we   were   hun - gry, ___   just ___   bare - ly   a - live. ___

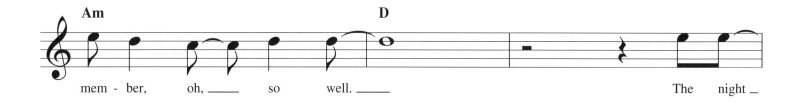

I   took   the   train   to   Rich - mond   that   fell; ___   it   was   a   time   I   re -

mem - ber,   oh, ___   so   well. ___   The   night ___

Chorus

_____ they drove old Dix - ie down _____ and all the

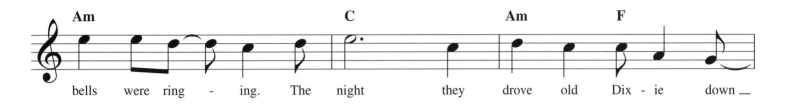

bells were ring - ing. The night they drove old Dix - ie down _

_____ and all the peo - ple were sing - ing. They went: Na na na

na na na, _____ na na na na na na _____ na na _ na.

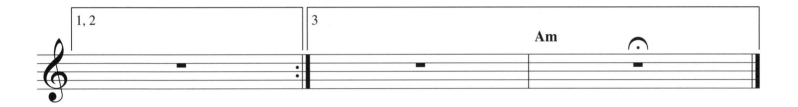

Additional Lyrics

2. Back with my wife in Tennessee, and one day she said to me,
   "Virgil, quick, come see. There goes Robert E. Lee."
   Now I don't mind, I'm chopping wood,
   And I don't care if the money's no good.
   Just take what you need and leave the rest,
   But they should never have taken the very best.
   Chorus

3. Like my father before me, I'm a working man.
   And like my brother before me, I took a rebel stand.
   But he was just eighteen, proud and brave,
   But a Yankee laid him in his grave.
   I swear by the blood below my feet,
   You can't raise a Caine back up when he's in defeat.
   Chorus

OCTOPUS'S GARDEN

Words and Music by
RICHARD STARKEY

I'd like to be _____ un - der the sea __

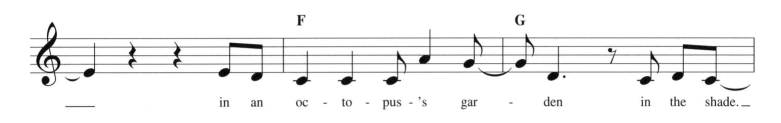

_____ in an oc - to - pus - 's gar - den in the shade. __

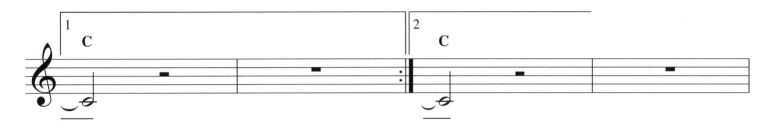

We would shout ____ and swim a - bout __

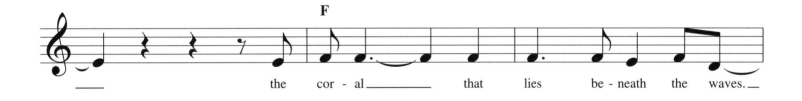

____ the cor - al _____ that lies be - neath the waves. __

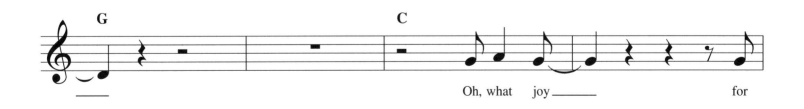

Oh, what joy _____ for

ev - 'ry girl and boy _____ know-ing ____ they're hap - py and they're

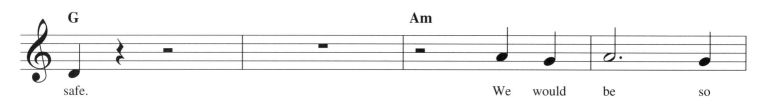

safe.   We would be so

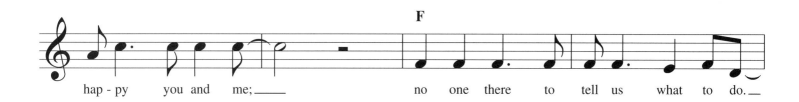

hap - py you and me;_____   no one there to tell us what to do._

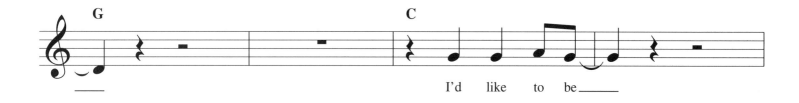

_____   I'd like to be_____

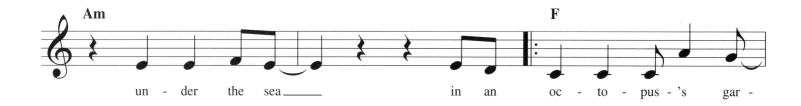

un - der the sea_____   in an oc - to - pus - 's gar -

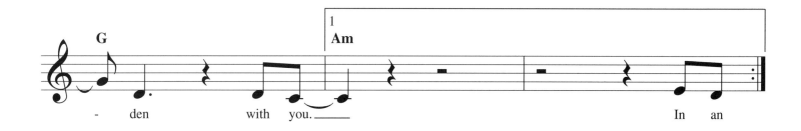

- den with you._____   In an

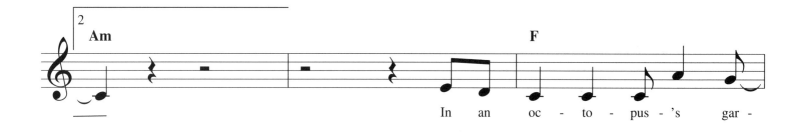

In an oc - to - pus - 's gar -

- den with you.   *(Instrumental)*

RED, RED WINE

Words and Music by
NEIL DIAMOND

ONE LOVE

Words and Music by
BOB MARLEY

Relaxed Reggae beat

One love, ___ one heart. ___ Let's get to-geth-er and

feel all right. { Hear the chil-dren cry-ing. (One love.) ___ Hear the chil-dren
As it was in the be-gin-ning, (One love.) ___ So shall it be in the
I'm plead-ing to ___ man-kind. (One love.) ___ Oh, Lord. _____

To Coda ⊕

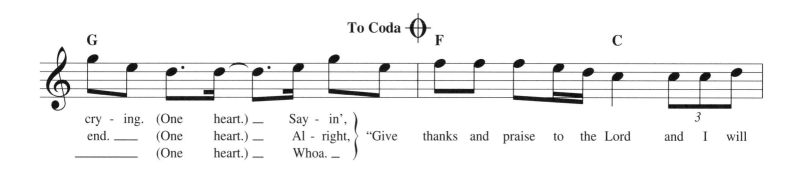

cry-ing. (One heart.) ___ Say-in', } "Give thanks and praise to the Lord and I will
end. ___ (One heart.) ___ Al-right,
_____ (One heart.) ___ Whoa. ___

feel all right." Say-in', "Let's get to-geth-er and

feel all right." { Whoa, whoa, whoa, whoa. Let them all pass all ___ their
One more thing. Let's get to-geth-er ___ to

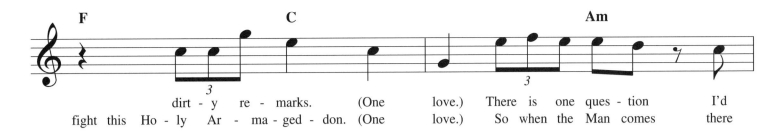

dirt - y re - marks. (One love.) There is one ques - tion I'd
fight this Ho - ly Ar - ma - ged - don. (One love.) So when the Man comes there

real - ly love to ask. ___ (One heart.) Is there a place ___ for the
will be no, no doom. __ (One song.) Have pit - y on those ___ whose chanc -

hope - less sin - ner who has hurt all man - kind just to
- es grow thin - ner. There ain't no hid - ing place from the

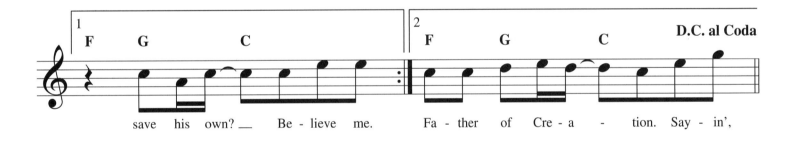

save his own? __ Be - lieve me. Fa - ther of Cre - a - tion. Say - in',

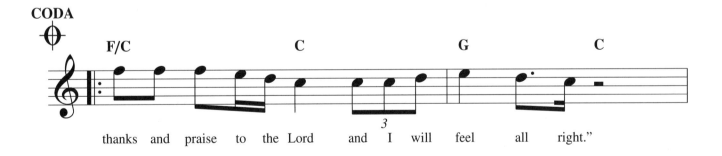

thanks and praise to the Lord and I will feel all right."

Let's get to - geth - er and feel all right. "Give feel all right.

PEACEFUL EASY FEELING

Words and Music by
JACK TEMPCHIN

Moderately fast

1. I like the way ___ your spar - klin' ear - rings ___
2., 3. *(See additional lyrics)*

lay   a - gainst ___ your   skin _____ so   brown. ___

And   I   wan - na   sleep   with   you ___ in   the

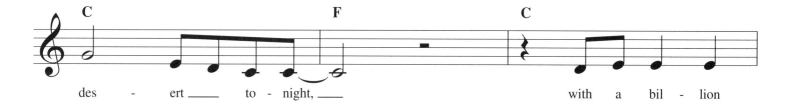

des - ert ___ to - night, ___   with   a   bil - lion

Chorus

stars   all   a - round. ___   'Cause   I   got   a   peace - ful ___

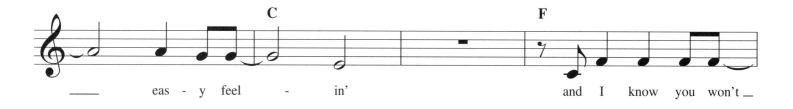

___ eas - y feel - in'   and   I   know   you   won't ___

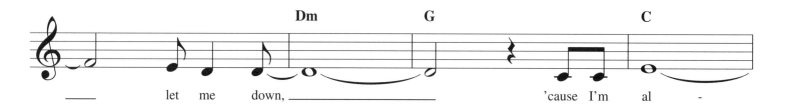

___   let   me   down, _____   'cause   I'm   al -

Additional Lyrics

2. And I found out a long time ago
   What a woman can do to your soul.
   Ah, but she can't take you any way
   You don't already know how to go.
   And I got a...*(To Chorus)*

3. I get this feeling I may know you
   As a lover and a friend.
   But this voice keeps whispering in my other ear;
   Tells me I may never see you again.
   'Cause I get a...*(To Chorus)*

PEGGY SUE

Words and Music by JERRY ALLISON,
NORMAN PETTY and BUDDY HOLLY

Brightly

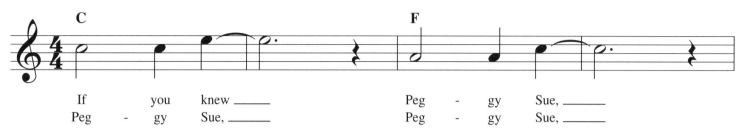

If you knew _____ Peg - gy Sue, _____
Peg - gy Sue, _____ Peg - gy Sue, _____

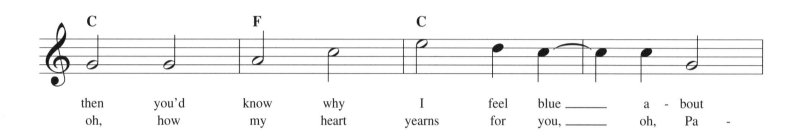

then you'd know why I feel blue _____ a - bout
oh, how my heart yearns for you, _____ oh, Pa -

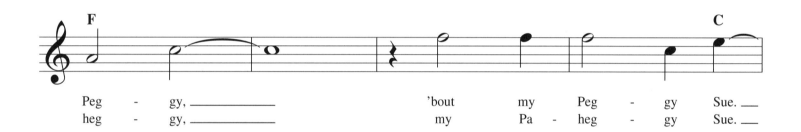

Peg - gy, _____ 'bout my Peg - gy Sue. _____
heg - gy, _____ my Pa - heg - gy Sue. _____

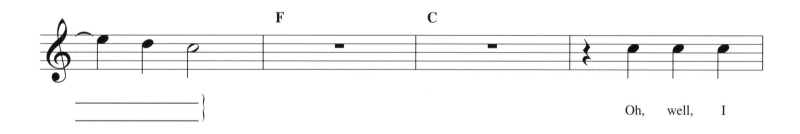

Oh, well, I

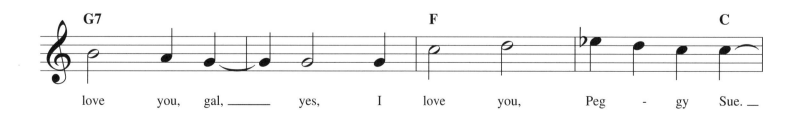

love you, gal, _____ yes, I love you, Peg - gy Sue. _____

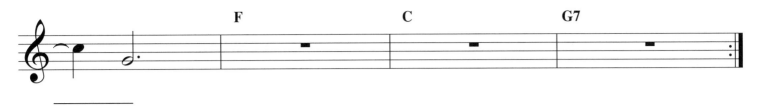

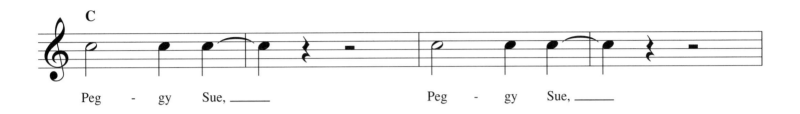

Peg - gy Sue, _____ Peg - gy Sue, _____

pret - ty, pret - ty, pret - ty, pret - ty Peg - gy Sue, ___

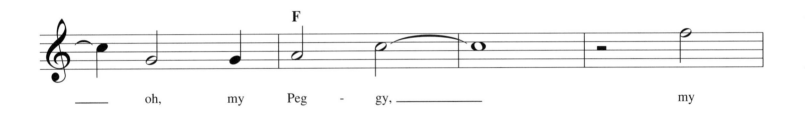

_____ oh, my Peg - gy, _____ my

Peg - gy Sue. _____

Oh, well, I love you, gal, _____ and I need you,

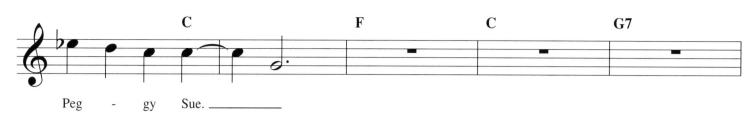

Peg - gy Sue. _____

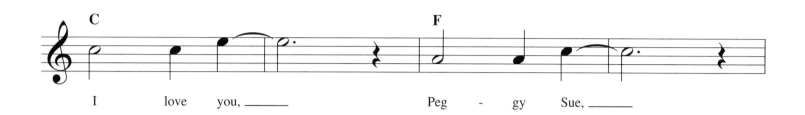

I love you, _____ Peg - gy Sue, _____

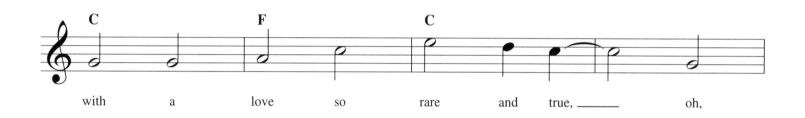

with a love so rare and true, _____ oh,

Peg - gy, _____ my Peg - gy Sue. ___

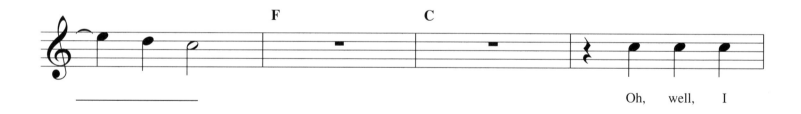

_____ Oh, well, I

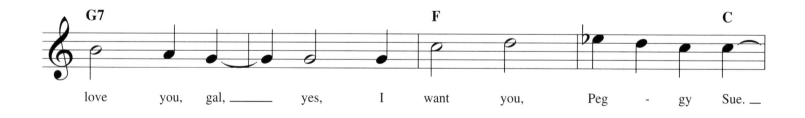

love you, gal, _____ yes, I want you, Peg - gy Sue. ___

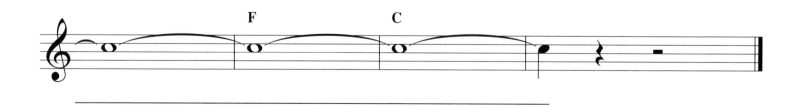

RUNAROUND SUE

Words and Music by ERNIE MARASCA
and DION DI MUCCI

Freely

Here's my sto - ry, it's sad but true; _____

it's a - bout a girl _____ that I once knew. _____ She took my love then

ran a - round with ev - 'ry sin - gle guy in town.

Moderately, with strong off-beat

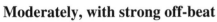

Hayp hayp bum - da ha - dy ha - dy, hayp hayp

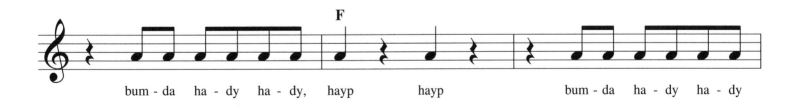

bum - da ha - dy ha - dy, hayp hayp bum - da ha - dy ha - dy

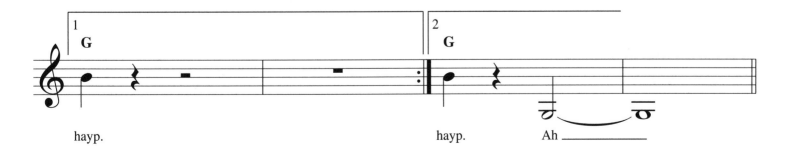

hayp. hayp. Ah _____

Now, peo - ple, let me put you wise: _____

G **N.C.** **C**

Sue goes ____ out with oth - er guys. Here's the mor - al and the sto - ry from the

Am

guy __ who knows, __ I fell in love and my love ___ still grows. __

F **G** **N.C.**

Ask an - y fool that she ev - er knew, __ they'll say keep a - way from - a

C

Run - a - round Sue. Hayp hayp bum - da ha - dy ha - dy,

Am **F**

hayp hayp bum - da ha - dy ha - dy, hayp hayp

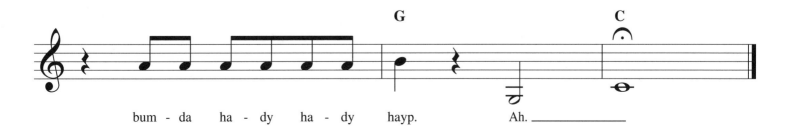

G **C**

bum - da ha - dy ha - dy hayp. Ah. _____

PINK HOUSES

Words and Music by
JOHN MELLENCAMP

Moderate Rock

There's a   black man   with a   black cat
young man   in a   T - shirt
peo - ple   and more   peo - ple.

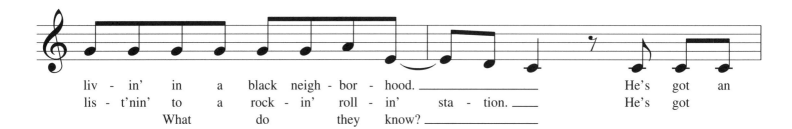

liv - in' in a black neigh - bor - hood. _____ He's got an
lis - t'nin' to a rock - in' roll - in' sta - tion. _____ He's got
What do they know? _____

in - ter - state ___ run - nin' through ___ his front yard. ___ You know, he
greas - y hair ___ and a greas - y smile ___ that says, "Lord,
Go to work ___ in some high - rise and va - ca - tion down at

thinks he's got it so good. _____ And there's a
this must be my des - ti - na - tion." 'Cause they
the Gulf of Mex - i - co. _____ And there's

wom - an in the kitch - en clean - in' up the eve - nin' slop. ___
told me when I was young - er, "Boy, you gon - na be Pres - i -
win - ners and there's los - ers, but they ain't no big deal. ___

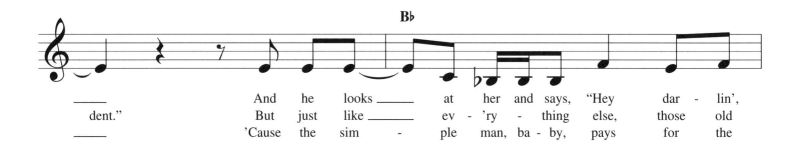

_____ And he looks ___ at her and says, "Hey dar - lin',
dent." But just like ___ ev - 'ry - thing else, those old
_____ 'Cause the sim - ple man, ba - by, pays for the

PLEASE MR. POSTMAN

Words and Music by ROBERT BATEMAN,
GEORGIA DOBBINS, WILLIAM GARRETT,
FREDDIE GORMAN and BRIAN HOLLAND

Moderately fast

Oh yes, wait a min - ute, Mis - ter Post - man.

Wait, _____ Mis - ter Post - man,

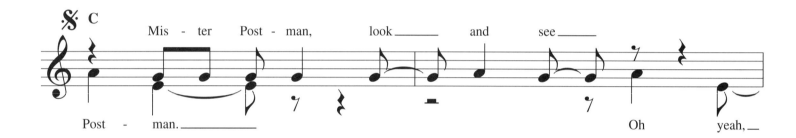

Mis - ter Post - man, look ____ and see ____

Post - man. _____ Oh yeah, __

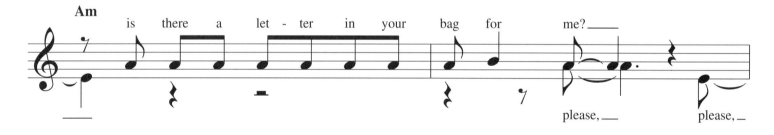

is there a let - ter in your bag for me? ____

please, ____ please, __

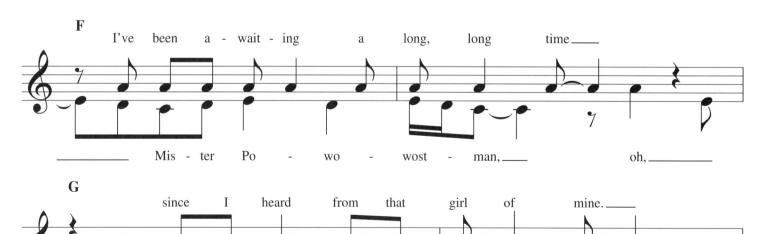

I've been a - wait - ing a long, long time ____

Mis - ter Po - wo - wost - man, ____ oh, _____

since I heard from that girl of mine. ____

yeah. _____

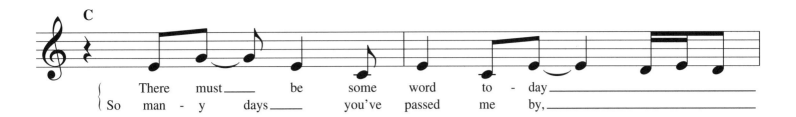

C

There must____ be some word to - day_____
So man - y days____ you've passed me by,_____

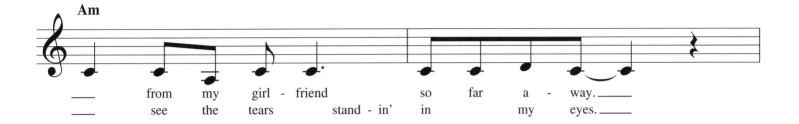

Am

___ from my girl - friend so far a - way.____
___ see the tears stand - in' in my eyes.____

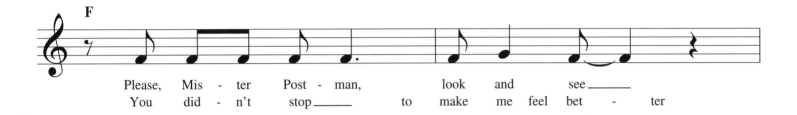

F

Please, Mis - ter Post - man, look and see____
You did - n't stop____ to make me feel bet - ter

To Coda $\oplus$

G

if there's a let - ter, a let - ter for me._____
by leav - ing me a

C

I've been stand - in' here____ wait - ing Mis - ter Post - man,

Am

so_____ pa - tient - ly_____

for just a card, or just a let - ter

D.S. al Coda

say - ing she's re - turn - ing home___ to me.___ Then Mis - ter

CODA

C

card or a let - ter, Mis - ter Post - man.___ Mis - ter Post - man, look___

___ and see___

Am

Is there a let - ter in your

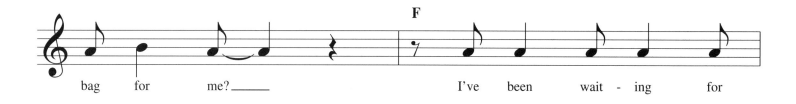

F

bag for me?___ I've been wait - ing for

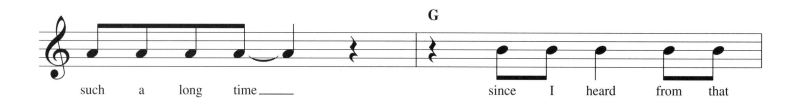

G

such a long time___ since I heard from that

girl - friend of mine. ___ You got - ta wait a min - ute, wait a min - ute,

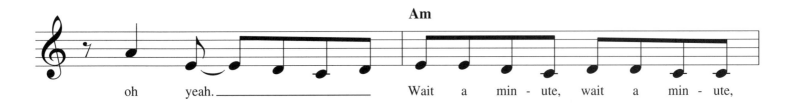

oh yeah. _____ Wait a min - ute, wait a min - ute,

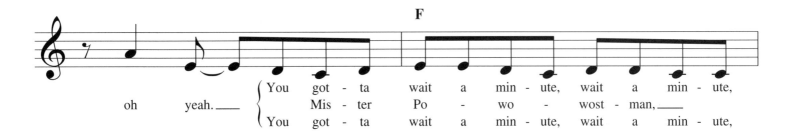

oh yeah. ___
{ You got - ta wait a min - ute, wait a min - ute,
Mis - ter Po - wo - wost - man, ___
You got - ta wait a min - ute, wait a min - ute, }

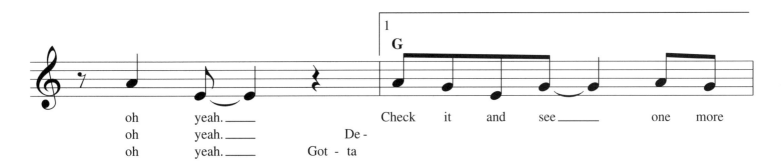

oh yeah. ___ Check it and see ___ one more
oh yeah. ___ De -
oh yeah. ___ Got - ta

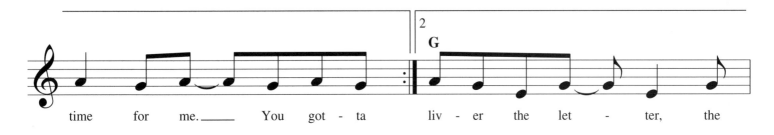

time for me. ___ You got - ta liv - er the let - ter, the

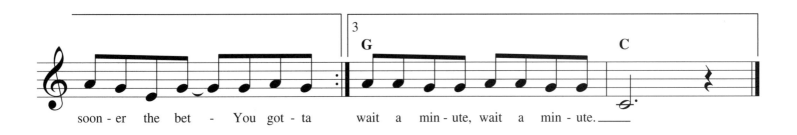

soon - er the bet - You got - ta wait a min - ute, wait a min - ute. ___

PUT A LITTLE LOVE IN YOUR HEART

Words and Music by JIMMY HOLIDAY,
RANDY MYERS and JACKIE DeSHANNON

Moderately

Think of your fel - low man, lend him a help - ing hand.
An - oth - er day ____ goes by, and still the chil - dren cry.

Put a lit - tle love ____ in your heart. ____
Put a lit - tle love ____ in your heart. ____ If

You see, it's get - ting late, oh, please don't hes - i - tate. ____
you want the world ____ to know, we won't let ha - tred grow. ____

Put a lit - tle love ____ in your heart. ____
Put a lit - tle love ____ in your heart. ____ And the world ____

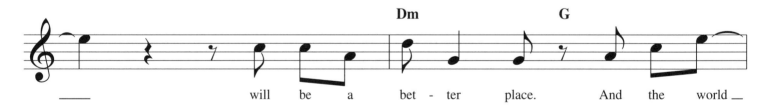

____ will be a bet - ter place. And the world ____

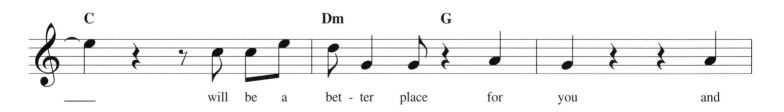

____ will be a bet - ter place for you and

me. You just wait ____ and see.

RUN AROUND

Words and Music by
JOHN POPPER

Brightly

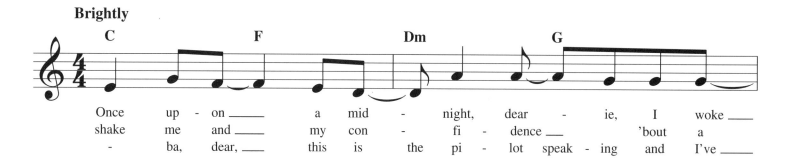

Once up-on _____ a mid - night, dear - ie, I woke _____
shake me and _____ my con - fi - dence _____ 'bout a
- ba, dear, _____ this is the pi - lot speak - ing and I've _____

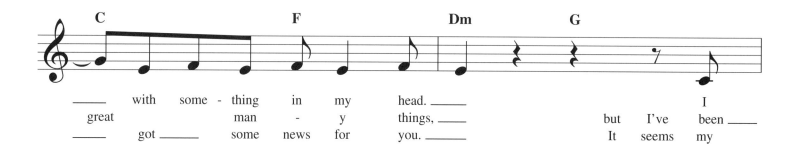

_____ with some - thing in my head. _____ I
great man - y things, _____ but I've been _____
_____ got _____ some news for you. _____ It seems my

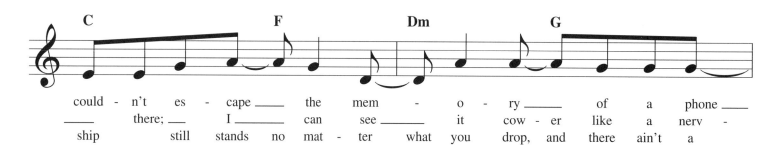

could - n't es - cape _____ the mem - o - ry _____ of a phone _____
_____ there; _____ I _____ can see _____ it cow - er like a nerv -
ship still stands no mat - ter what you drop, and there ain't a

_____ call and of _____ what you said. _____ Like a
ous ma - gi - cian wait - ing in the wings. _____ Or a bad _____
whole lot that you can do. Oh sure, the

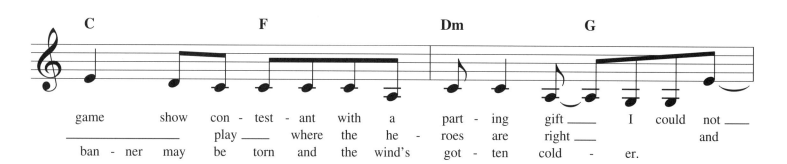

game show con - test - ant with a part - ing gift _____ I could not _____
play _____ where the he - roes are right _____ and
ban - ner may be torn and the wind's got - ten cold - er.

not   with - out   a   cer - tain   de - gree _____   of   fear _____   of _____
soon,   if   we're   luck - y,   we'd   be   un - a - ble   to   tell   what's ___
love   you   to   the   point   you   can   no   long - er   take.   Well,   all   right,

what   will   be _____   with   you   and   me. _____   I   still _____
yours   and   mine. ___   The   fish - ing's   fine, ____   and   it   does -
o - kay,   so   be   that   way.   I

_____   can   see _____   things,   hope - ful - ly. _____
n't   have   to   rhyme ___   so   don't   you   feed   me   a   line. ___   But   you, _____
hope   and   pray   that   there's   some - thing   left   to   say.

_____   why _____   you   wan - na

give   me   a   run _____   a - round? _____   Is _____   it   a   sure -

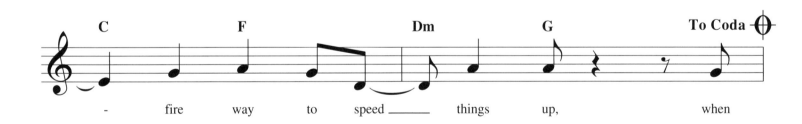

To Coda ⊕

- fire   way   to   speed _____   things   up,   when

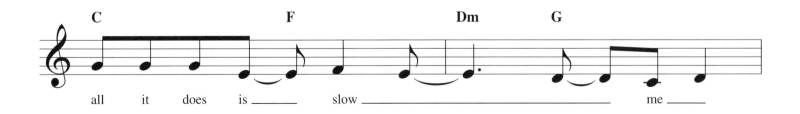

all   it   does   is _____   slow _____   me _____

SHOULD I STAY OR SHOULD I GO

Words and Music by MICK JONES
and JOE STRUMMER

Moderately bright

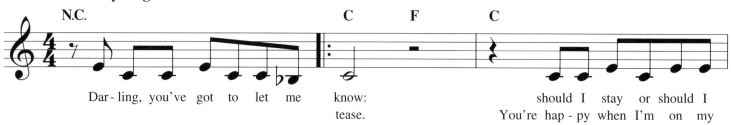

Dar - ling, you've got to let me know:
tease.
should I stay or should I
You're hap - py when I'm on my

go?
knees.
If you say that you are mine, __
One day is fine and next is black. __

I'll be here till the end of time.
So if you want me off your back,
So you've got to let me
well, come on and let me

know: _____
know: _____
should I stay or should I go?
should I stay or should I go?

1 C N.C.
It's al - ways tease, tease,

2 C N.C.
Should I stay or should I

Double-time feel
C   F
(D.S. only) ¿Me de - bo ir o que - dar-
go now?

C   **F**

me?   *¿Me de - bo ir o que - dar -*

Should I stay or should I go now?

C   **F**   **E♭**

me?   *Si me voy ___ va pe - li -*

If I go, there will be trou - ble.

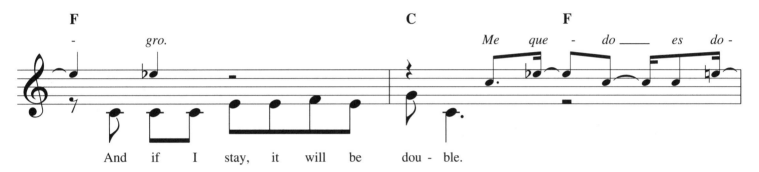

F   **C**   **F**

- gro.   *Me que - do ___ es do -*

And if I stay, it will be dou - ble.

C   **G7**   **To Coda**

- ble.   *Me tie - nes que de -*

So, come on and let me know. ___

End double-time feel

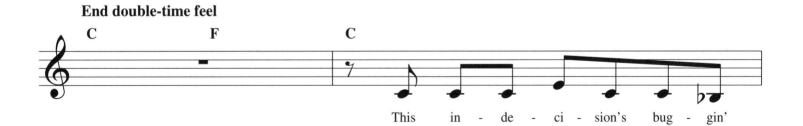

C   **F**   **C**

This in - de - ci - sion's bug - gin'

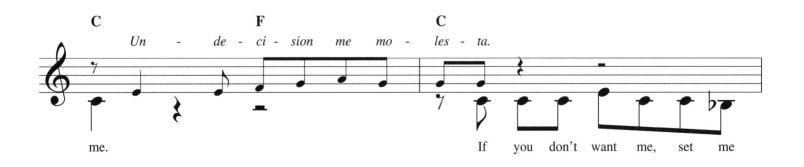

C   **F**   **C**

Un - de - ci - sion me mo - les - ta.

me.   If you don't want me, set me

158

SOMEBODY TO LOVE

Words and Music by
DARBY SLICK

Moderately fast

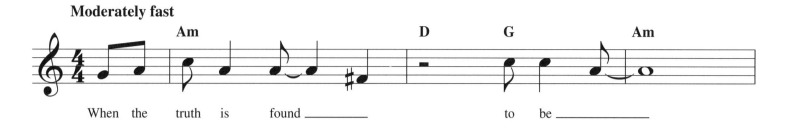

When the truth is found _____ to be _____

lies, and all of the joy _____ with - in you _____

___ dies, don't you want some - bod - y to love? _

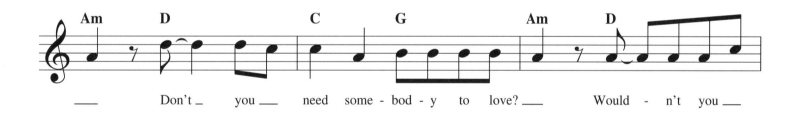

___ Don't _ you _ need some - bod - y to love? ___ Would - n't you ___

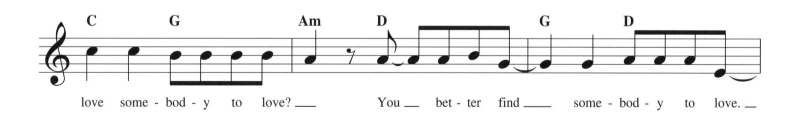

love some - bod - y to love? ___ You _ bet - ter find _____ some - bod - y to love. ___

___ Love. _   *Guitar solo*

SO YOU WANT TO BE A ROCK AND ROLL STAR

Words and Music by ROGER McGUINN
and CHRIS HILLMAN

Moderately fast

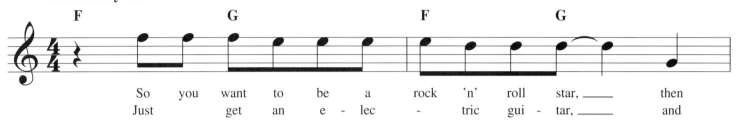

So you want to be a rock 'n' roll star, ___ then
Just get an e - lec - tric gui - tar, ___ and

lis - ten now ___ to what I've ___ got to say. ___
take some time ___ and learn ___ how to play. ___

And when your hair's ___ combed right ___ and your

pants fit tight, ___ it's gon - na be all right. ___

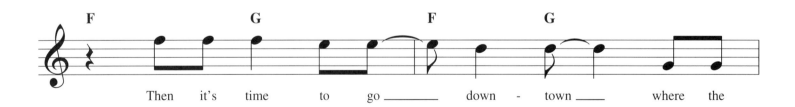

Then it's time to go ___ down - town ___ where the

a - gent man ___ won't let you down. ___

SPARKS FLY

Words and Music by
TAYLOR SWIFT

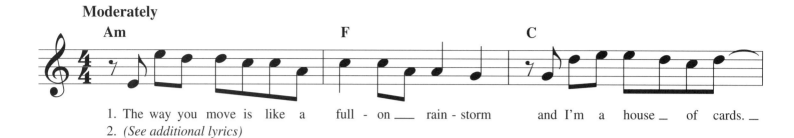

1. The way you move is like a full - on __ rain - storm and I'm a house __ of cards. __
2. *(See additional lyrics)*

__ You're the kind of reck - less that should send me run - ning, but I

kind - a know __ that I won't get far. __ And you stood __ there in front __

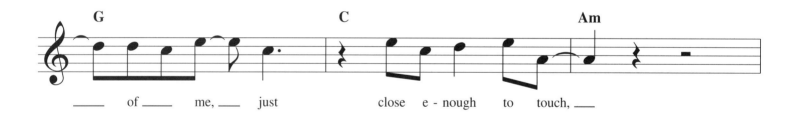

__ of __ me, __ just close e - nough to touch, __

close e - nough to hope __ you could - n't see __ what I was think - ing __ of. __

__ Drop ev - 'ry - thing now, __ meet __ me in the pour - ing rain. __

_____ the lights _____ go _____ wild. _____ Just keep on keep-ing your eyes _____

_____ on me. _____ It's just wrong e-nough to make it feel _____ right. _____ And

lead me up the stair - case. Won't _____ you whis - per soft _____ and slow? _____

_____ I'm cap - ti - vat - ed by _____ you, ba - by, like a

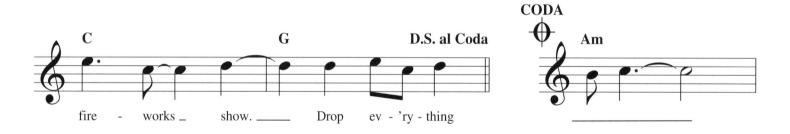

fire - works _____ show. _____ Drop ev - 'ry - thing

And the sparks _____ fly. _____

Additional Lyrics

2. My mind forgets to remind me
You're a bad idea.
You touch me once and it's really something.
You find I'm even better than you imagined I would be.
I'm on my guard for the rest of the world,
But with you, I know it's no good.
And I could wait patiently,
But I really wish you would...

SOUTHERN CROSS

Words and Music by STEPHEN STILLS,
RICHARD CURTIS and MICHAEL CURTIS

Moderately fast

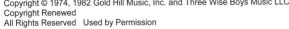

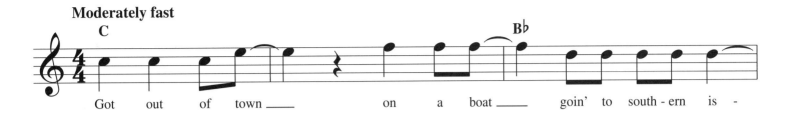

Got out of town ___ on a boat ___ goin' to south-ern is-

- lands.   Sail-ing a reach   be-fore a fol-low-ing

sea.   She was mak-ing for the trades ___ on the

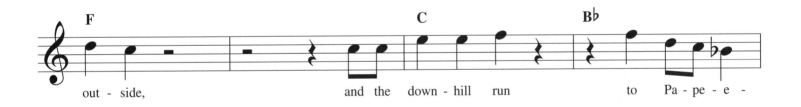

out-side,   and the down-hill run   to Pa-pe-e-

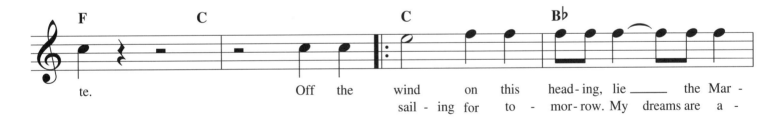

te.   Off the wind on this head-ing, lie ___ the Mar-
sail-ing for to - mor-row. My dreams are a-

que - sas.   We got eight-y feet ___ of the wa-ter-line,
dy - ing.   And my love is an an-chor tied to you,

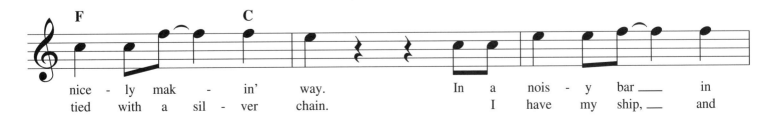

nice-ly mak - in' way.   In a nois-y bar ___ in
tied with a sil - ver chain.   I have my ship, ___ and

SPANISH EYES

Words by CHARLES SINGLETON and EDDIE SNYDER
Music by BERT KAEMPFERT

Moderately

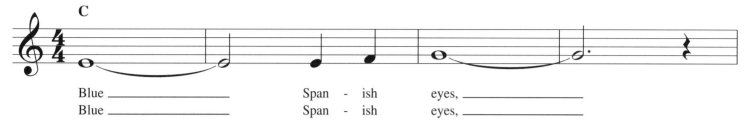

Blue _____ Span - ish eyes, _____
Blue _____ Span - ish eyes, _____

tear - drops are fall - ing from your Span - ish eyes. _____
pret - ti - est eyes in all of Mex - i - co. _____

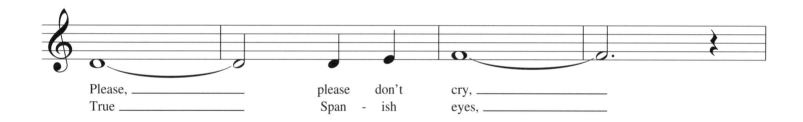

Please, _____ please don't cry, _____
True _____ Span - ish eyes, _____

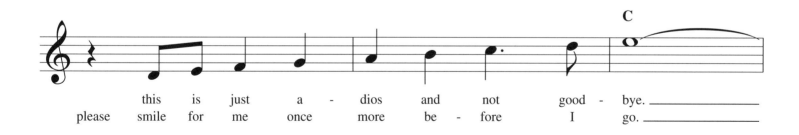

this is just a - dios and not good - bye. _____
please smile for me once more be - fore I go. _____

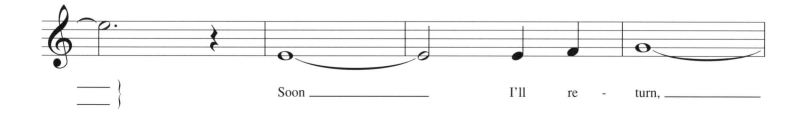

_____ Soon _____ I'll re - turn, _____

bring - ing   you   all   the   love   your   heart   can

hold. _____   Please _____   say   sí

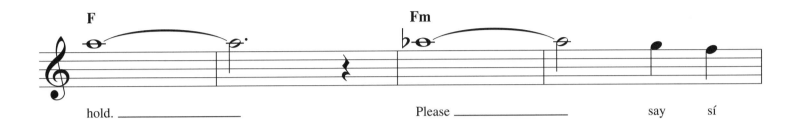

sí, _____   say   you   and   your   Span - ish

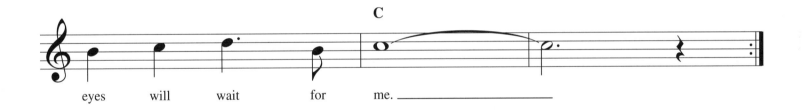

eyes   will   wait   for   me. _____

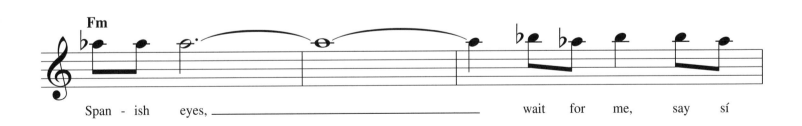

Span - ish   eyes, _____   wait   for   me,   say   sí

sí. _____

SPOOKY

Words and Music by J.R. COBB,
BUDDY BUIE, HARRY MIDDLEBROOKS
and MIKE SHAPIRO

Moderately

In the cool of the eve-ning when ev - 'ry-thing is get - tin' kind of
al - ways keep me guess-ing, I nev - er seem to know what you are
Instrumental
If you de-cide ___ you'd bet - ter stop this lit - tle game that you are

groov - y,   I call you up and ask you if you'd
think - ing.   And if a fel - ler looks at you, it's for

play - ing,   I'm gon - na tell you all the things my

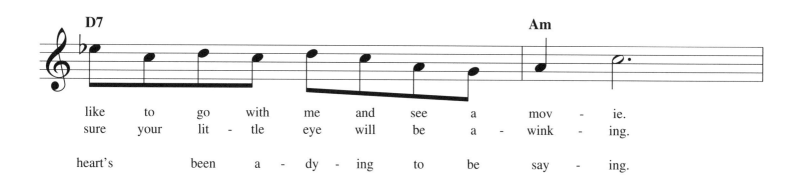

like to go with me and see a mov - ie.
sure your lit - tle eye will be a - wink - ing.

heart's been a - dy - ing to be say - ing.

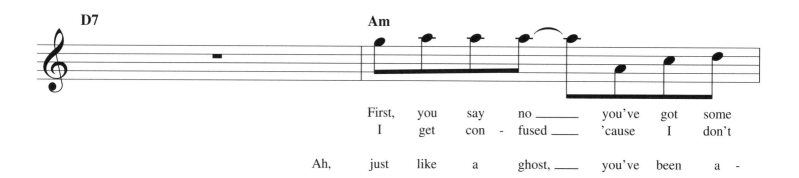

First, you say no ___ you've got some
I get con - fused ___ 'cause I don't

Ah, just like a ghost, ___ you've been a -

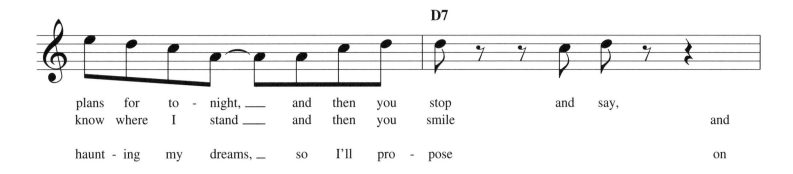

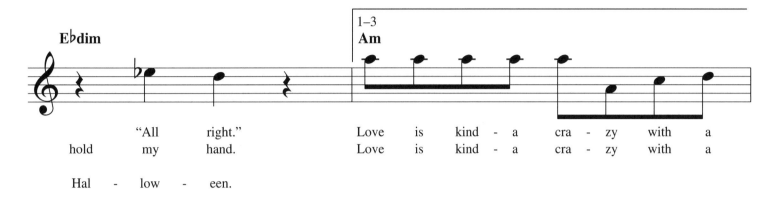

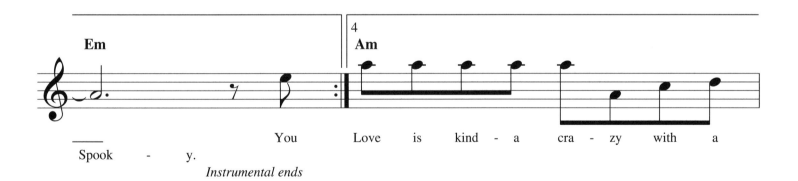

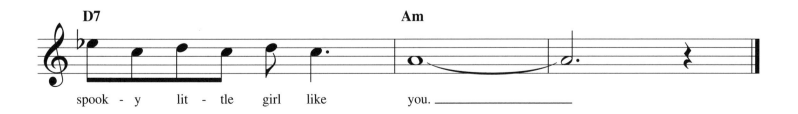

STAND BY ME

Words and Music by JERRY LEIBER,
MIKE STOLLER and BEN E. KING

When the night _____ has come   and the land is

dark   and the moon _____ is the on - ly _____ light we'll

see,   no, I won't be a - fraid, no, _____ I _____

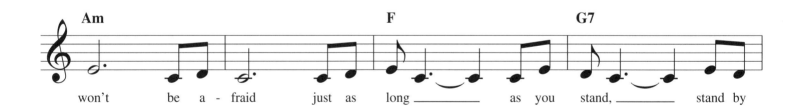

won't   be a - fraid   just as long _____ as you stand, _____ stand by

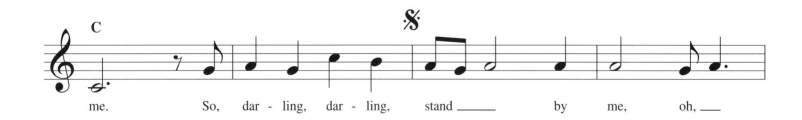

me.   So, dar - ling, dar - ling, stand _____ by me, oh, _____

stand _____ by me, oh, stand, _____ stand by me,

stand by me. _____ If the sea _____ that we look up -

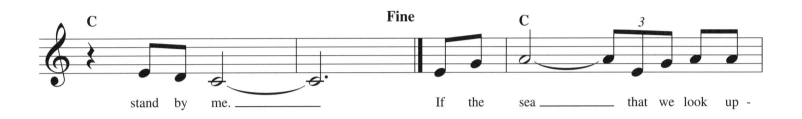

on should tum - ble and fall, or the moun - tain _____ should

crum - ble _____ in the sea, I won't cry, I won't

cry, no, _____ I _____ won't shed a tear just as

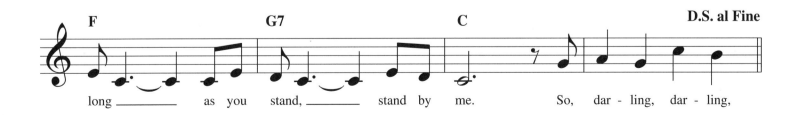

long _____ as you stand, _____ stand by me. So, dar - ling, dar - ling,

STUCK IN THE MIDDLE WITH YOU

Words and Music by GERRY RAFFERTY
and JOE EGAN

Moderately

Well, I don't _____ know why I came here to - night. _____ I got the
stuck in the mid - dle with you _____ and I'm won -
Tryin' to make some sense of it all _____ but I can
Instrumental

feel - in' that some - thing ain't right. _____ I'm so scared _
- d'ring what it is I should do. _____ It's so hard _
see it makes no _____ sense at all. _____ Is it cool _

F7

_____ in case I fall off my chair _____ and I'm won -
_____ to keep this smile from my face. _____ Los - ing con -
_____ to go to sleep on the floor? _____ You don't think _

C

- d'ring how I'll get down the stairs. _____ ⎫
- trol I'm all o - ver the place. _____ ⎬ (1.–3.) Clowns _
_____ that I can take an - y - more. _____ ⎭ (4.) *Instrumental*

G   **B♭**   **F7**

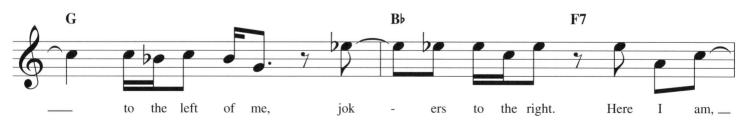

_____ to the left of me, jok - ers to the right. Here I am, _

STAYIN' ALIVE
from the Motion Picture SATURDAY NIGHT FEVER

Words and Music by BARRY GIBB,
ROBIN GIBB and MAURICE GIBB

Well, you can tell _____ by the way I use _____ my walk, _____ I'm a wom-
_____ get _____ low and I _____ get high _____ and if I _____

- an's man: no time to talk. _____
_____ can't get ei - ther, I real - ly try. Got the

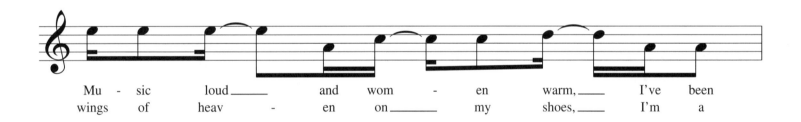

Mu - sic loud _____ and wom - en warm, _____ I've been
wings of heav - en on _____ my shoes, _____ I'm a

kicked a - round _____ since I _____ was born. _____ And now it's
danc - in' man _____ and I just can't lose. _____ You know it's

all right. ___ It's O. K. _____ And you may look ___ the oth - er way. _____
all right. ___ It's O. K. _____ I'll live to see ___ an - oth - er day. ___

We can try___ to un-der-stand___ the New York Times'___ ef - fect___ on man.___

Am

Wheth - er you're a broth - er or wheth - er you're a moth - er, you're stay -

- in' a - live,_____ stay - in' a - live._____

Feel the cit - y break - in' and ev - 'ry - bod - y shak - in' and we're

stay - in' a - live,___ stay - in' a - live.___ Ah, ha, ha, ha,

stay - in' a - live,___ stay - in' a - live.___ Ah, ha, ha, ha,

stay-in' a - live.

Well now, I

Life go - in' no - where. Some - bod - y help me.

Some - bod - y help me, yeah.

Life go - in' no - where. Some - bod - y help me, yeah.

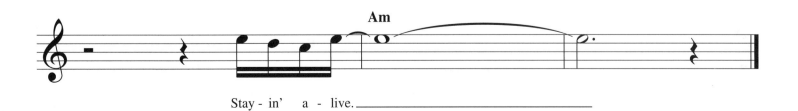

Stay - in' a - live.

SUNDOWN

Words and Music by
GORDON LIGHTFOOT

Moderately

1. I can see her ly - ing back in her sat - in dress ____ in a
2.–4. *(See additional lyrics)*

room where you do ____ what you don't con - fess. ____

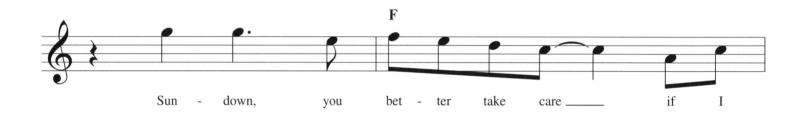

Sun - down, you bet - ter take care ____ if I

find you been creep - ing 'round ____ my back stairs. ____

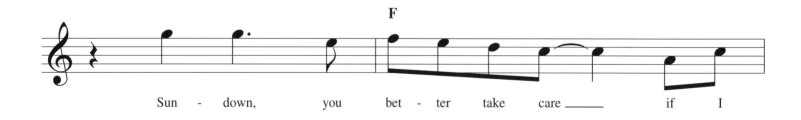

Sun - down, you bet - ter take care ____ if I

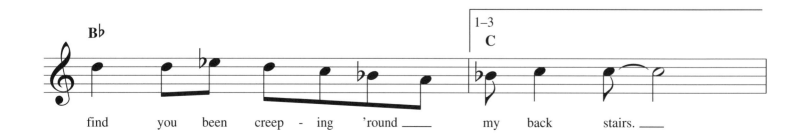

find you been creep - ing 'round ____ my back stairs. ____

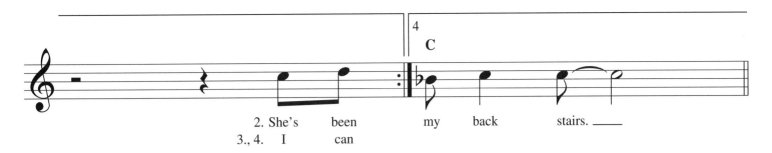

2. She's been my back stairs. _____

3., 4. I can

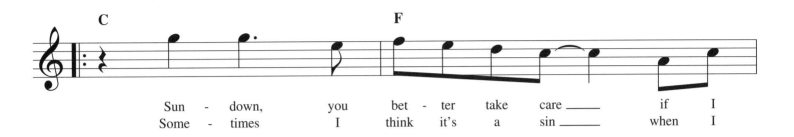

Sun - down, you bet - ter take care _____ if I

Some - times I think it's a sin _____ when I

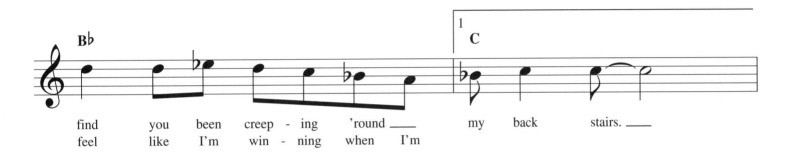

find you been creep - ing 'round _____ my back stairs. _____

feel like I'm win - ning when I'm

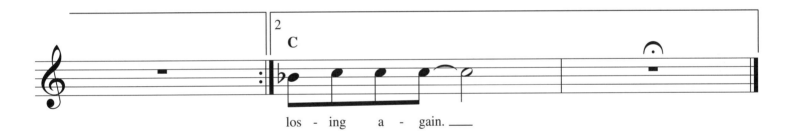

los - ing a - gain. _____

Additional Lyrics

2. She's been looking like a queen in a sailor's dream,
And she don't always say what she really means.
Sometimes I think it's a shame when I get feeling better when I'm feeling no pain.
Sometimes I think it's a shame when I get feeling better when I'm feeling no pain.

3. I can picture ev'ry move that a man could make.
Getting lost in her loving is your first mistake.
Sundown, you better take care if I find you been creeping 'round my back stairs.
Sometimes I think it's a sin when I feel like I'm winning when I'm losing again.

4. I can see her looking fast in her faded jeans.
She's a hard-loving woman, got me feeling mean.
Sometimes I think it's a shame when I get feeling better when I'm feeling no pain.
Sundown, you better take care if I find you been creeping 'round my back stairs.

SUPERCALIFRAGILISTICEXPIALIDOCIOUS
from Walt Disney's MARY POPPINS

Words and Music by RICHARD M. SHERMAN
and ROBERT B. SHERMAN

Brightly

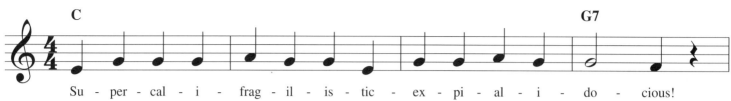

Su - per - cal - i - frag - il - is - tic - ex - pi - al - i - do - cious!

E - ven though the sound of it is some - thing quite a - tro - cious.

If you say it loud e - nough, you'll al - ways sound pre - co - cious.

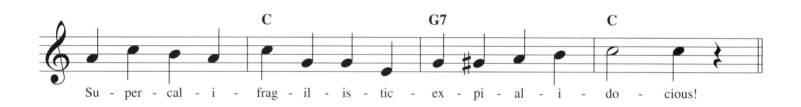

Su - per - cal - i - frag - il - is - tic - ex - pi - al - i - do - cious!

Um did - dle did - dle did - dle, um did - dle ay! Um did - dle did - dle did - dle, um did - dle ay! { Be- / He / So

cause I was a - fraid to speak when I was just a lad, me
trav - eled all a - round the world and ev - 'ry - where he went he'd
when the cat has got your tongue, there's no need for dis - may. Just

SURFIN' SAFARI

Words and Music by BRIAN WILSON
and MIKE LOVE

Bright Rock

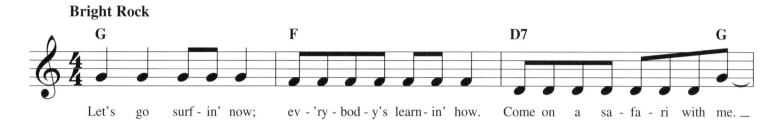

Let's go surf-in' now; ev-'ry-bod-y's learn-in' how. Come on a sa-fa-ri with me. _

Ear-ly in the morn-in' we'll be start-in' out; ___ some
ang-lin' in La-gu-na and ___ Cerro A-zul. ___ They're

hon-eys will be com-in' a-long. ___ We're load-in' up our wood-y with the
kick-in' out in Do-he-ny, too. ___ I tell you surf-in's run-nin' wild, it's get-tin'

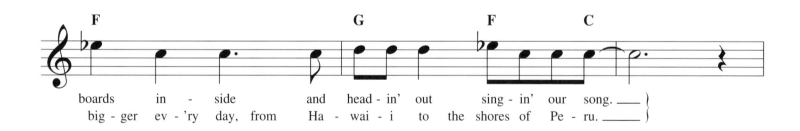

boards in-side and head-in' out sing-in' our song. ___
big-ger ev-'ry day, from Ha-wai-i to the shores of Pe-ru. ___

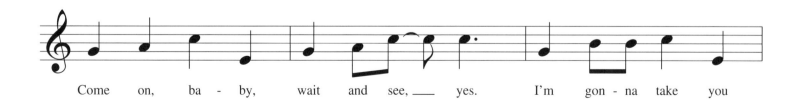

Come on, ba-by, wait and see, ___ yes. I'm gon-na take you

surf - in' with me. ___ Lone - some ba - by, wait and see, ___ yes.

I'm gon - na take you surf - in' with me. ___ Let's go surf - in' now;

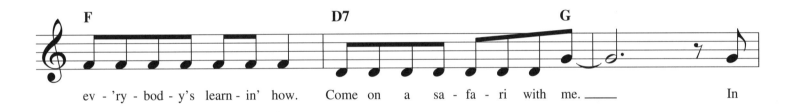

ev - 'ry - bod - y's learn - in' how. Come on a sa - fa - ri with me. ___ In

Hunt - ing - ton and Ma - li - bu they're shoot - in' the pier. ___ In Rin - con, they're walk - in' the nose. ___

___ We're go - in' on sa - fa - ri to the is - lands this year. ___ So if you're

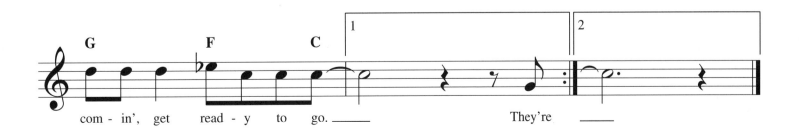

com - in', get read - y to go. ___ They're ___

SUSIE-Q

Words and Music by DALE HAWKINS,
STAN LEWIS and ELEANOR BROADWATER

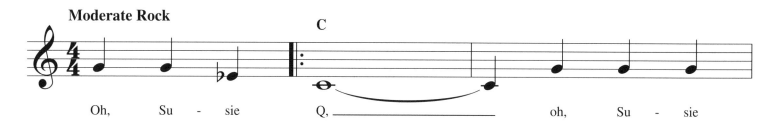

Oh, Su - sie Q, _____ oh, Su - sie

Q, oh, Su - sie Q, how I love

you, my Su - sie Q.

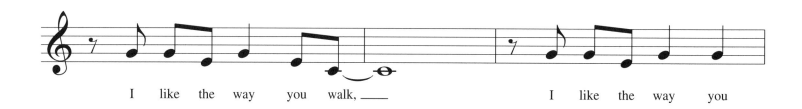

I like the way you walk, ____ I like the way you

talk. I like the way you walk, I like the way you

talk, my Su - sie Q. Oh, Su - sie Q. _____

SUZANNE

Words and Music by
LEONARD COHEN

Moderately, flowing

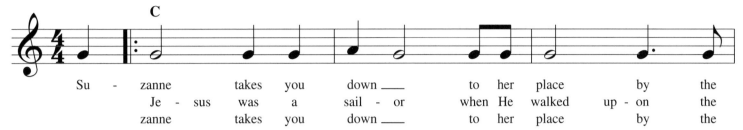

Su - zanne takes you down ___ to her place by the
Je - sus was a sail - or when He walked up - on the
zanne takes you down ___ to her place by the

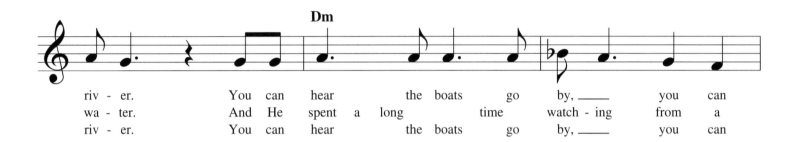

riv - er. You can hear the boats go by, ___ you can
wa - ter. And He spent a long time watch - ing from a
riv - er. You can hear the boats go by, ___ you can

spend the night for - ev - er. ___ And you know that she's half
lone - ly wood - en tow - er. ___ And when He knew for
spend the night for - ev - er. ___ And the sun pours down like

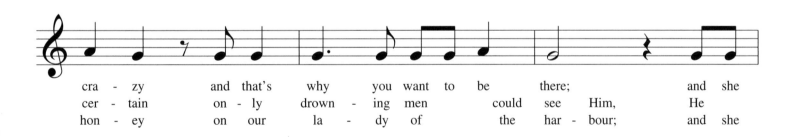

cra - zy and that's why you want to be there; and she
cer - tain on - ly drown - ing men could see Him, He
hon - ey on our la - dy of the har - bour; and she

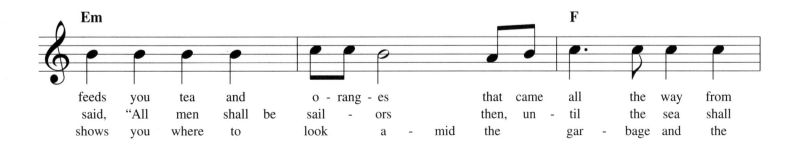

feeds you tea and o - rang - es that came all the way from
said, "All men shall be sail - ors then, un - til the sea shall
shows you where to look a - mid the gar - bage and the

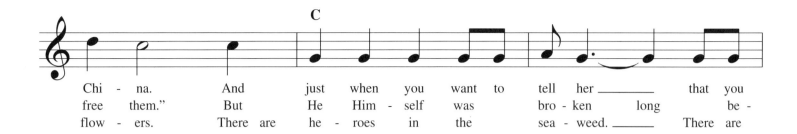

C

Chi - na. And just when you want to tell her _____ that you
free them." But He Him - self was bro - ken long be -
flow - ers. There are he - roes in the sea - weed. _____ There are

Dm

have no love to give her, _____ she gets you on her
fore the sky would o - pen. _____ For - sak - en, al - most
chil - dren in the morn - ing. _____ They are lean - ing out for

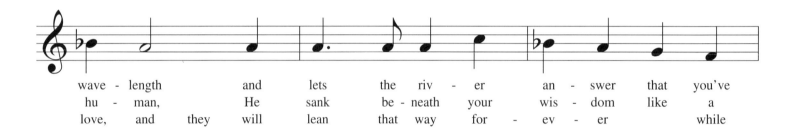

wave - length and lets the riv - er an - swer that you've
hu - man, He sank be - neath your wis - dom like a
love, and they will lean that way for - ev - er while

C

al - ways _____ been her lov - er. _____
stone. _____
Su - zanne _____ holds her mir - ror. _____

Em

And you want to trav - el with her, _____ and you
And you want to trav - el with Him, _____ and you
And you want to trav - el with her, _____ and you

SWEET HOME ALABAMA

Words and Music by RONNIE VAN ZANT,
ED KING and GARY ROSSINGTON

Moderately slow

1. Big wheels keep on turn-ing   car-ry me home to see my

kin.   Sing-ing songs a-bout the South-land

I miss ole 'Bam-y once a-gain. ___   *(And I think it's a sin.)*

2. Well, I heard Mis-ter Young sing a-bout her.

Well, I heard ole Neil ___ put her down.   Well, I hope Neil Young will re-

mem-ber   a South-ern man don't need him a-round an-y-how. ___

Sweet home Al-a-bam-a,   where the skies are so

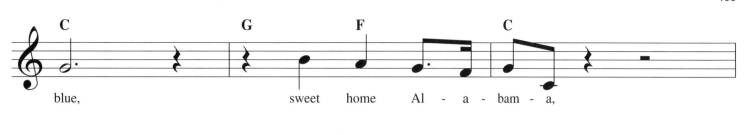

blue,   sweet home Al - a - bam - a,

Lord, I'm com - ing home to   you.   3. In Bir - ming - ham they love the
4. *(See additional lyrics)*

Gov' - nor.   Boo! boo!   boo! Now we all did what we could do. _____

Now Wa - ter - gate does not both - er me.   Does your con - science both - er

Chorus

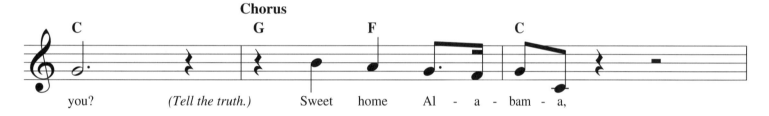

you?   *(Tell the truth.)*   Sweet home Al - a - bam - a,

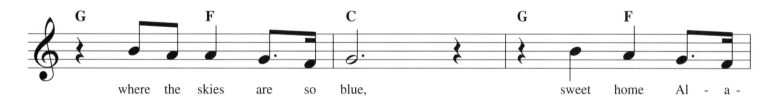

where the skies are so blue,   sweet home Al - a -

bam - a,   Lord, I'm com - ing home to   you.

Additional Lyrics

4. Now Muscle Shoals has got the Swampers
And they've been known to pick a tune or two
Lord, they get me off so much
They pick me up when I'm feeling blue
Now how about you.
Chorus

SWEET JANE

Words and Music by
LOU REED

Medium Rock

1. Stand - in' on the cor - ner,   suit - case in my
2., 3. *(See additional lyrics)*

hand.   Jack is in his cor - set, Jane is in her vest,

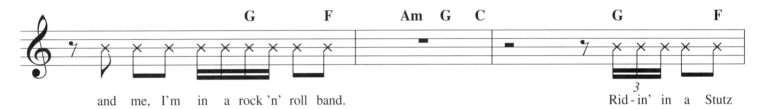

and me, I'm in a rock 'n' roll band.   Rid - in' in a Stutz

Bear Cat, Jim.   You know,   those were diff -'rent times.

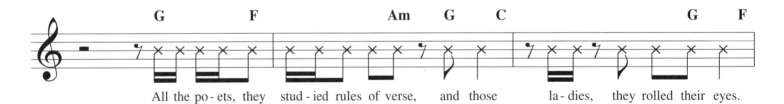

All the po - ets, they stud - ied rules of verse,   and those   la - dies, they rolled their eyes.

1, 2

Sweet   Jane. _____   Sweet   Jane. _

_____   Sweet   Jane. _____

Additional Lyrics

2. Jack, he is a banker,
   And Jane, she is a clerk,
   And both of them save their monies.
   And when they come home from work,
   Sittin' down by the fire,
   The radio does play
   The March of the Wooden Soldiers,
   And you can hear Jack say...
   Sweet Jane. Sweet Jane. Sweet Jane.

3. Some people, they like to go dancin',
   And other people, they have to work.
   And there's even some evil mothers,
   Well, they're gonna tell you that everything is just dirt.
   You know that women never really faint.
   And that villians always blink their eyes,
   That children are the only ones who blush,
   And that life is just to die.

A TEENAGER IN LOVE

Words and Music by DOC POMUS
and MORT SHUMAN

Moderately fast

Each time we have a quar - rel   it al - most
One day I feel so hap - py;   next day I

breaks my heart.   'Cause I am so a - fraid
feel so sad.   I guess I'll learn to take

that we will have to part.
the good ____ with the bad.   Each night I

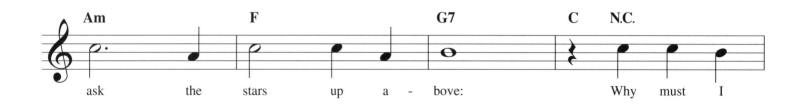

ask the stars up a - bove: Why must I

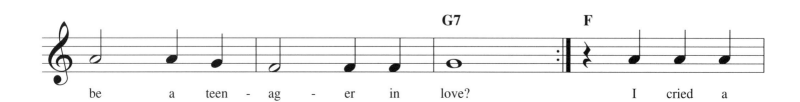

be a teen - ag - er in love?   I cried a

tear   for   no - bod - y   but   you.   I'll   be   a

lone - ly   one   if   you   should   say   we're   through.   If   you   want   to

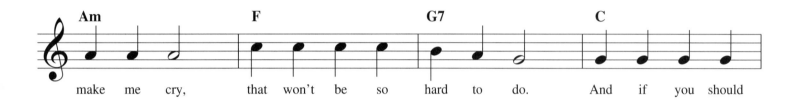

make   me   cry,   that   won't   be   so   hard   to   do.   And   if   you   should

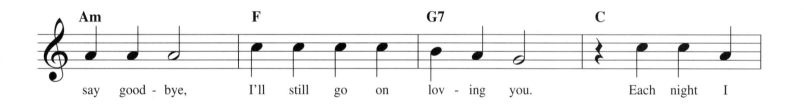

say   good - bye,   I'll   still   go   on   lov - ing   you.   Each   night   I

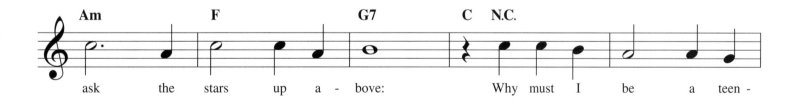

ask   the   stars   up   a - bove: Why   must   I   be   a   teen -

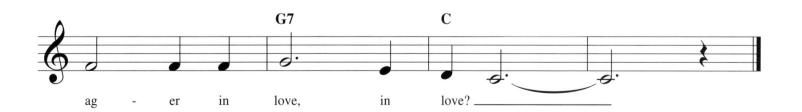

ag - er   in   love,   in   love? _____

THAT'LL BE THE DAY

Words and Music by JERRY ALLISON,
NORMAN PETTY and BUDDY HOLLY

Well, you give me all your lov - in' and your tur - tle-dov - in', all ___

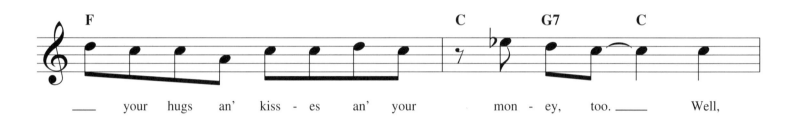

___ your hugs an' kiss - es an' your mon - ey, too. ___ Well,

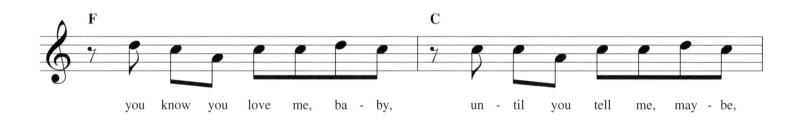

you know you love me, ba - by, un - til you tell me, may - be,

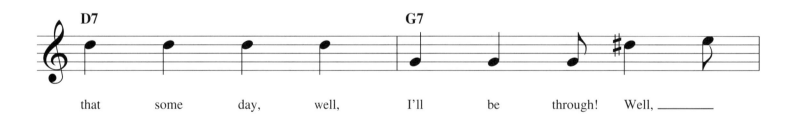

that some day, well, I'll be through! Well, ___

that - 'll be the day, when you say good - bye, yes, ___

199

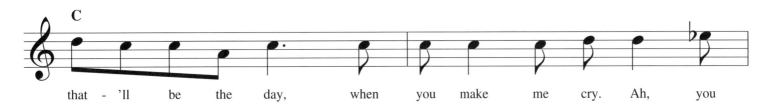

that-'ll be the day, when you make me cry. Ah, you

say you're gon - na leave, you know it's a lie, _____ 'cause

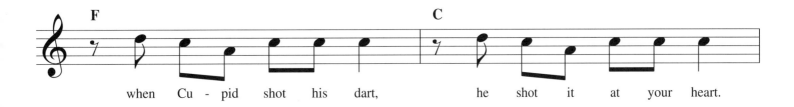

that-'ll be the day _____ when I die. _____ Well,

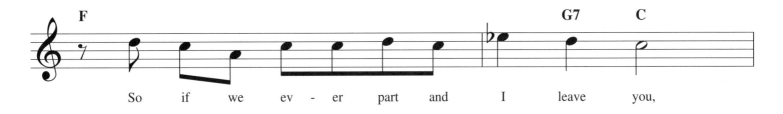

when Cu - pid shot his dart, he shot it at your heart.

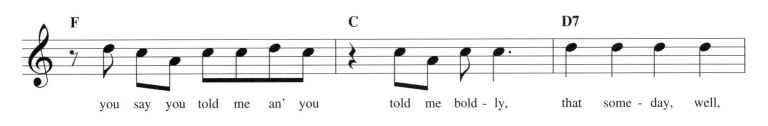

So if we ev - er part and I leave you,

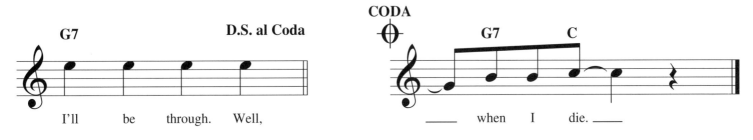

you say you told me an' you told me bold - ly, that some - day, well,

I'll be through. Well,

_____ when I die. _____

THIS MAGIC MOMENT

Words and Music by DOC POMUS
and MORT SHUMAN

This mag - ic mo - ment, _____ so dif - f'rent and so

new, was like an - y oth - er _____ un - til

I kissed you. _____ And then it hap - pened. _____

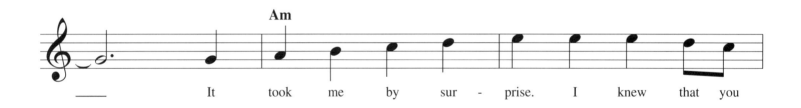

_____ It took me by sur - prise. I knew that you

felt it, too, _____ by the look in your eyes, _____

_____ sweet - er than ___ wine, _____ soft - er than a

THE TIMES THEY ARE A-CHANGIN'

Words and Music by
BOB DYLAN

1. Come gath - er 'round peo - ple wher - ev - er you roam _____
2.–5. *(See additional lyrics)*

_____ and ad - mit that the wa - ters a - round you have

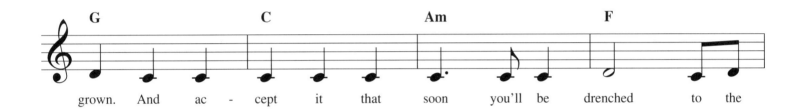

grown. And ac - cept it that soon you'll be drenched to the

bone, _____ if your time to you is worth

sav - in' _____ then you bet - ter start swim - min' or you'll

sink like a stone, for the times they are a -

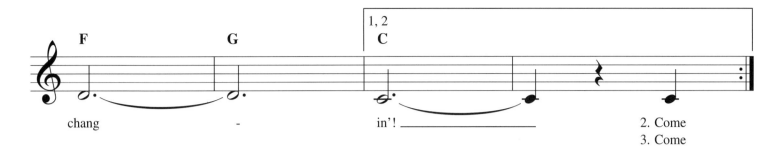

chang - in'! _____ 2. Come
3. Come

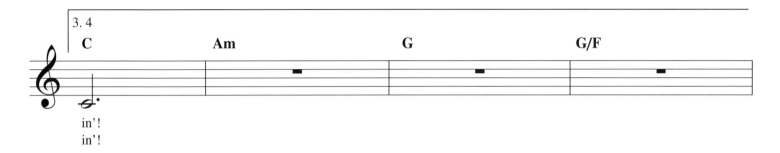

in'!
in'!

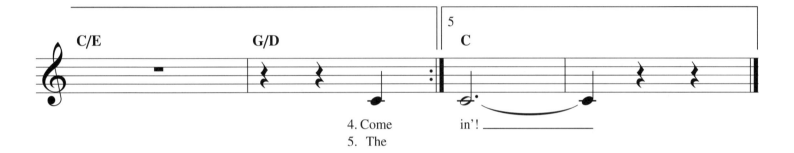

4. Come in'! _____
5. The

Additional Lyrics

2. Come writers and critics
Who prophesy with your pen
And keep your eyes wide
The chance won't come again.
And don't speak too soon
For the wheel's still in spin,
And there's no tellin' who
That it's namin'.
For the loser now
Will be later to win
For the times they are a-changin'.

3. Come senators, congressmen
Please heed the call
Don't stand in the doorway
Don't block up the hall.
For he that gets hurt
Will be he who has stalled,
There's a battle
Outside and it's ragin'.
It'll soon shake your windows
And rattle your walls
For the times they are a-changin'!

4. Come mothers and fathers,
Throughout the land
And don't criticize
What you can't understand.
Your sons and your daughters
Are beyond your command,
Your old road is
Rapidly agin'.
Please get out of the new one
If you can't lend your hand
For the times they are a-changin'!

5. The line it is drawn
The curse it is cast
The slow one now will
Later be fast.
As the present now
Will later be past,
The order is rapidly fadin'.
And the first one now
Will later be last
For the times they are a-changin'!

TWO PRINCES

Words and Music by
SPIN DOCTORS

Moderately fast

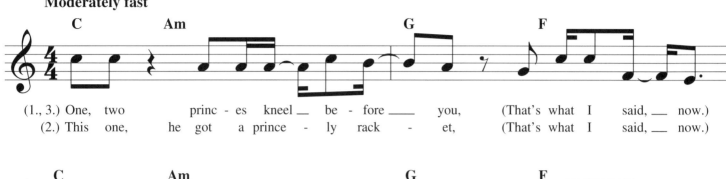

(1., 3.) One, two   princ - es kneel __ be - fore ___ you, (That's what I   said, __ now.)
(2.) This one,   he got   a prince - ly rack - et, (That's what I   said, __ now.)

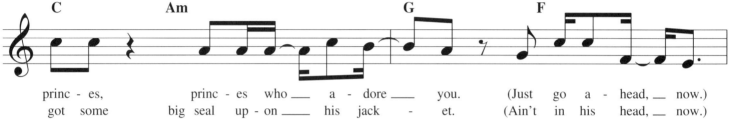

princ - es,   princ - es who __ a - dore ___ you. (Just go a - head, __ now.)
got some   big seal up - on ___ his jack - et. (Ain't in his   head, __ now.)

One has   dia - monds in ___ his pock - ets; (That's some   bread, __ now.)
Mar - ry him,   your fa - ther will __ con - done ___ you. (How 'bout   that, __ now.) You

this   one,   he wants to buy __ you rock - ets. (Ain't in his   head, __ now.)
mar - ry me,   your fa - ther will __ dis - own ___ you. (He'll eat his   hat, ___ now.)

To Coda ⊕

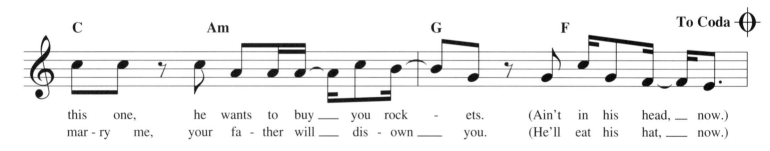

1

Yeah, _____ yeah,   yeah. _____   (Di   di   ga

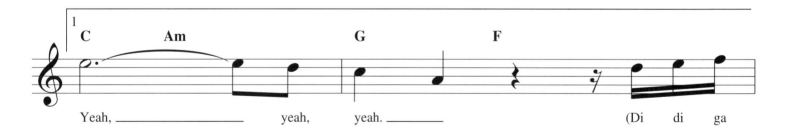

dip.   Di dip dip di dip. Ba dee - dle - ee   di ba du ba du ba du ba du ba du ba du ba du ba.)

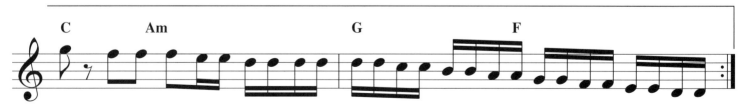

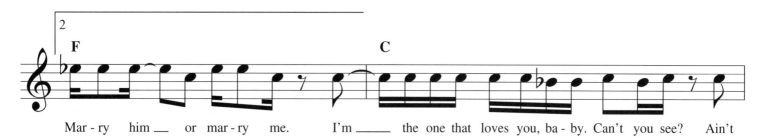

Mar - ry him __ or mar - ry me. I'm ____ the one that loves you, ba - by. Can't you see? Ain't

got no fu - ture or a fam - 'ly tree, __ but I know what a prince and lov - er ought to be. __

I know what a prince and lov - er ought to be. __ Said, if you want to call __ me, ba-

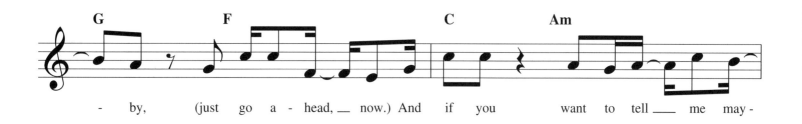

- by, (just go a - head, __ now.) And if you want to tell __ me may-

- be, (just go a - head, __ now.) And if you wan - na buy __ me flow-

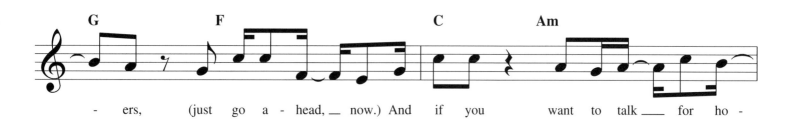

- ers, (just go a - head, __ now.) And if you want to talk __ for ho -

D.C. al Coda

- urs, (just go a - head, __ now.)

CODA

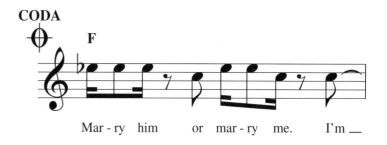

Mar - ry him or mar - ry me. I'm __

____ the one that loves you, ba - by. Can't you see? __ I ain't got no fu - ture or a fam -'ly tree, __ but

I know what a prince and lov - er ought to be. __ I know what a prince and lov - er ought to be. ____

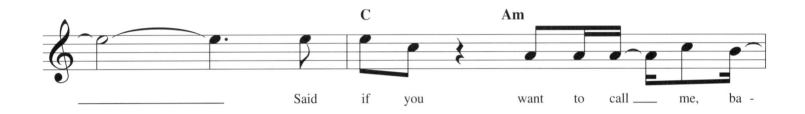

_____ Said if you want to call __ me, ba -

- by, (just go a - head, __ now.) And if you want to tell __ me may -

- be, (just go a - head, __ now.) And if you wan - na buy __ me flow -

- ers (just go a - head, __ now.) And if you want to talk __ for ho -

- urs, (just go a - head, __ now.)

TODAY WAS A FAIRYTALE

Words and Music by
TAYLOR SWIFT

Moderately fast

1. To - day   was   a   fair - y - tale.   You   were   the   prince.   I   used   to   be   a
3. *(See additional lyrics)*

dam - sel   in   dis - tress.   You   took   me   by   the   hand   and   you   picked   me   up   at

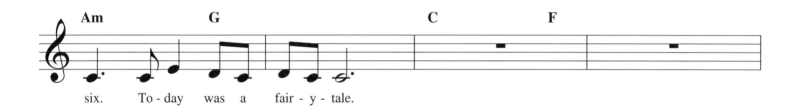

six.   To - day   was   a   fair - y - tale.

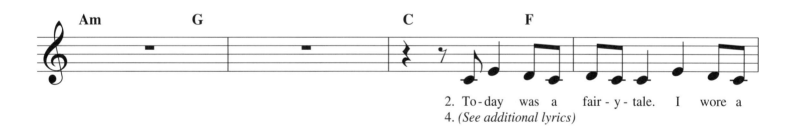

2. To - day   was   a   fair - y - tale.   I   wore   a
4. *(See additional lyrics)*

dress,   you   wore   a   dark   grey   t - shirt.   You   told   me   I   was

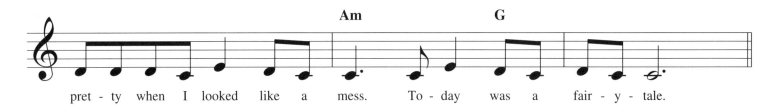

pret - ty when I looked like a mess. To - day was a fair - y - tale.

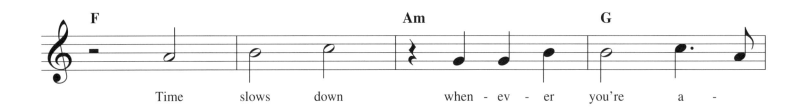

Time slows down when - ev - er you're a -

round. _____ But can you

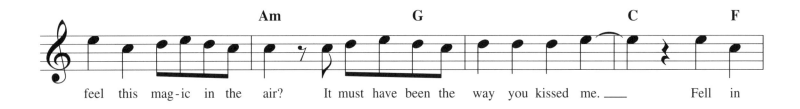

feel this mag - ic in the air? It must have been the way you kissed me. ____ Fell in

love when I saw you stand - in' there. It must -'ve been the way to - day was a

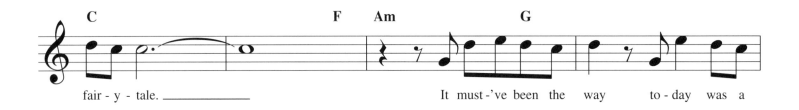

fair - y - tale. _____ It must -'ve been the way to - day was a

fair - y - tale. _____ Time

slows down when - ev - er you're a - round. I can

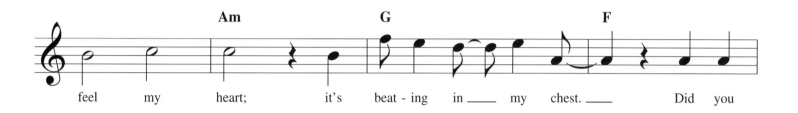

feel my heart; it's beat - ing in ___ my chest. ___ Did you

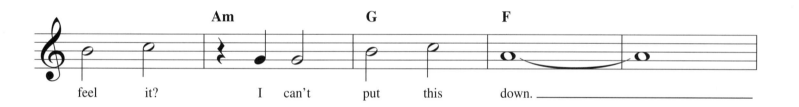

feel it? I can't put this down. _____

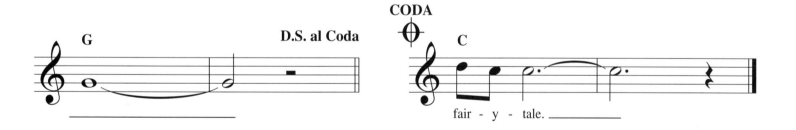

CODA

D.S. al Coda

fair - y - tale. _____

Additional Lyrics

3. Today was a fairytale.
   You've got a smile
   Takes me to another planet.
   Every move you make,
   Everything you say is right.
   Today was a fairytale.

4. Today was a fairytale.
   All that I can say
   Is now it's getting so much clearer.
   Nothing made sense
   Till the time I saw your face.
   Today was a fairytale.

TOES

Words and Music by SHAWN MULLINS,
ZAC BROWN, WYATT DURRETTE
and JOHN DRISKELL HOPKINS

I got my toes in the wa - ter, ass ____ in the sand, ____ not a wor -

- ry in the world, ____ a cold beer in my hand. ____ Life is good ____

____ to - day, life is good ____ to - day. Well, the plane ____

____ touched down ____ just a - bout ____ three o' - clock ____ and the cit -
____ flew by ____ like a drunk ____ Fri - day night ____ as the sum -

- y's still ____ on my mind. ____
- mer drew ____ to an end. ____ Bi -

ki - nis and palm ____ trees danced ____ in my head, ____ I was still ____
They can't be - lieve ____ that I just could - n't leave, ____ and I bid ____

play.
play.
(Instrumental)

D.S. al Coda

The four days ___

A - di - os and va - ya con

CODA

(Spoken:) Just gonna drive up by the lake and put my

ass in a lawn ___ chair, toes ___ in the clay, ___ not a wor -

- ry in the world, ___ a P - B - R on the way. ___ Life is good ___ to - day,

life is good ___ to - day.

TURN THE PAGE

Words and Music by
BOB SEGER

Moderately

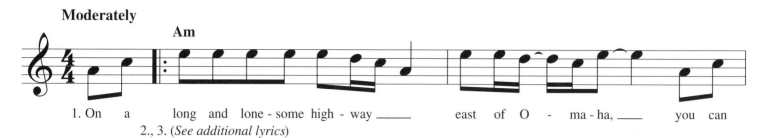

1. On a long and lone-some high-way ___ east of O - ma - ha, ___ you can
2., 3. (*See additional lyrics*)

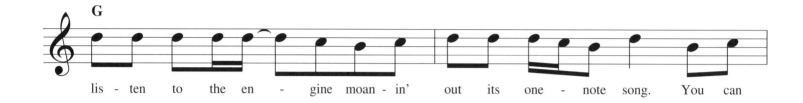

lis - ten to the en - gine moan - in' out its one - note song. You can

think a - bout ___ the wom - an or the girl you knew ___ the night ___ be -

fore. ___ But your thoughts will soon be wan - der - in', ___ the

way they al - ways do, ___ when you're rid - in' six - teen hours ___ and there's

noth - in' much ___ to do. ___ And you don't feel much like rid - in'; you just

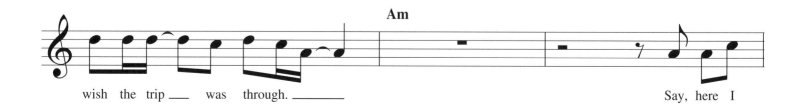

wish the trip ___ was through. ___ Say, here I

Additional Lyrics

2. Well, you walk into a restaurant strung out from the road,
   And you feel the eyes upon you as you're shakin' off the cold;
   You pretend it doesn't bother you but you just want to explode.
   Most times you can't hear 'em talk, other times you can,
   All the same old clichés, "Is that a woman or a man?"
   And you always seem outnumbered, you don't dare make a stand.
   Chorus

3. Out there in the spotlight you're a million miles away.
   Every ounce of energy you try to give away
   As the sweat pours out your body like the music that you play.
   Later in the evening as you lie awake in bed
   With the echoes from the amplifiers ringing in your head,
   You smoke the day's last cigarette remembering what she said.
   Chorus

WANTED DEAD OR ALIVE

Words and Music by JON BON JOVI
and RICHIE SAMBORA

Moderately slow

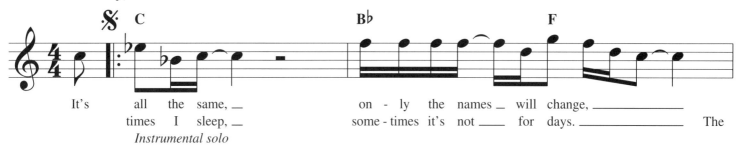

It's all the same, __ on - ly the names __ will change, ___ The
times I sleep, __ some - times it's not __ for days. ___
Instrumental solo

ev - 'ry day, ___ it seems we're wast - ing a - way. __ An -
peo - ple I meet al - ways go their sep - 'rate ways. Some -

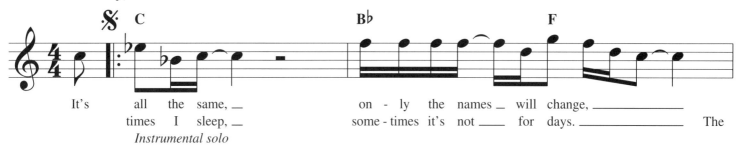

oth - er place, ___ where the fac - es are __ so cold, I'd
times you tell __ the day ___ by the bot - tle that __ you drink. And

drive all night, ___ just to get back __ home. __
times when you're a - lone, ___ all you do is think. __ I'm a
Solo ends

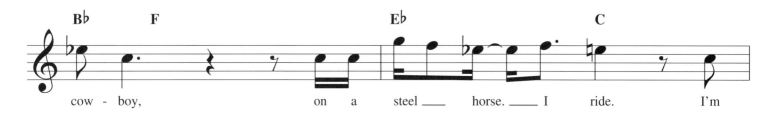

cow - boy, on a steel __ horse. __ I ride. I'm

To Coda ⊕

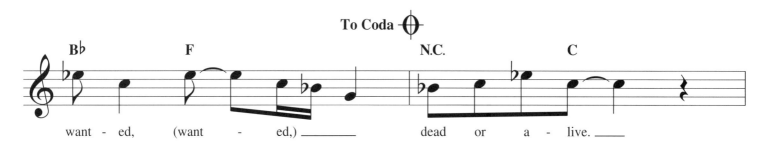

want - ed, (want - ed,) ___ dead or a - live. __

WALKING IN THE SUNSHINE

Words and Music by
ROGER MILLER

Brightly

Walk-ing in the sun - shine, sing-ing a lit - tle sun - shine song,

put a smile up - on your face as if there's noth - ing wrong.

Think a - bout a good time had a long time a - go; think a - bout for - get - ting a - bout your

wor - ries and your woes, walk - ing in the sun - shine, sing - ing a lit - tle sun - shine

song. La la la la la dee oh,

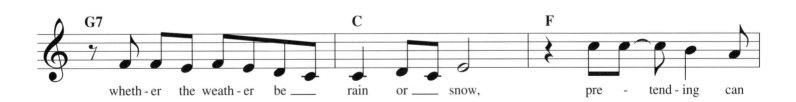

wheth - er the weath - er be rain or snow, pre - tend - ing can

make it real, a snow - y pas - ture, a green and grass - y field.

WIDE OPEN SPACES

Words and Music by
SUSAN GIBSON

Moderately fast

Who does-n't know what I'm talk-ing a-bout? __

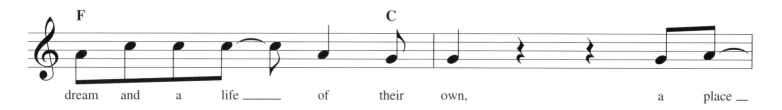

Who's nev-er left home, who's __ nev-er struck out   to find a

dream and a life __ of their own,   a place __

__ in the clouds, __ a foun-da-tion of stone? __

Man-y pre-cede and man-y will fol-low,
She trav-eled this road __ as __ a child, __

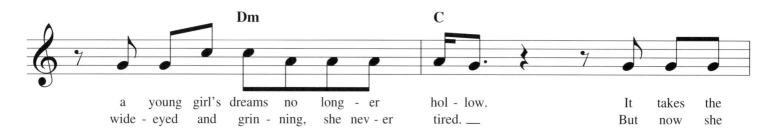

a young girl's dreams no long-er hol-low.   It takes the
wide-eyed and grin-ning, she nev-er tired. __   But now she

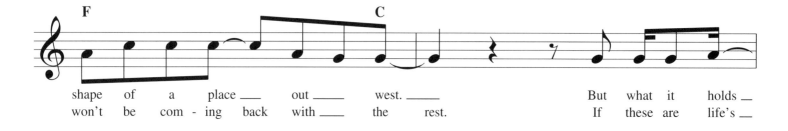

shape of a place __ out __ west. __   But what it holds __
won't be com-ing back with __ the rest.   If these are life's __

222

THE WAY YOU DO THE THINGS YOU DO

Words and Music by WILLIAM "SMOKEY" ROBINSON
and ROBERT ROGERS

WILD THING

Words and Music by
CHIP TAYLOR

Moderately slow Rock/Funk

(1.,3.)Wild thing, you make my heart sing. You make ev-
(2.) *Instrumental*

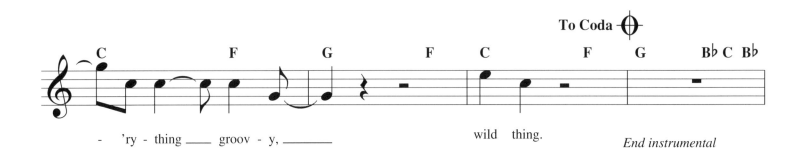

- 'ry - thing ___ groov - y, ___ wild thing. *End instrumental*

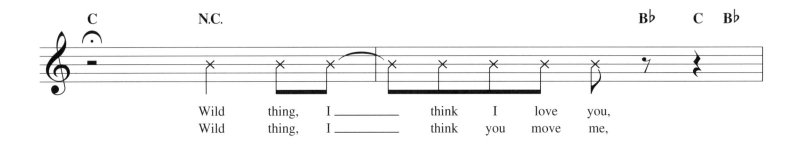

Wild thing, I ___ think I love you,
Wild thing, I ___ think you move me,

but I wan - na know ___ for sure. Come on and
but I wan - na know ___ for sure. Come on and

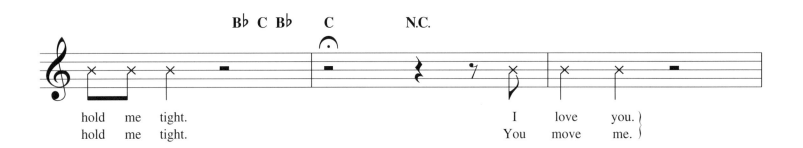

hold me tight. I love you.
hold me tight. You move me.

(Instrumental)

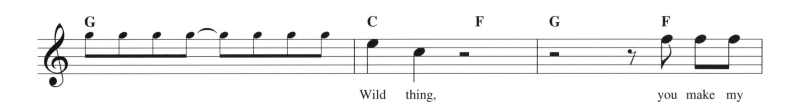

Wild thing, you make my

heart sing. You make ev - 'ry - thing ___ groov - y, ___

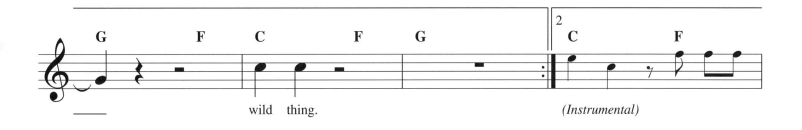

___ wild thing. *(Instrumental)*

D.C. al Coda

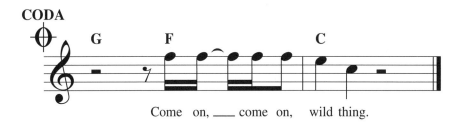

CODA

Come on, ___ come on, wild thing.

WONDERFUL TONIGHT

Words and Music by
ERIC CLAPTON

Moderate Ballad

It's late in the eve - ning: she's won - d'ring what clothes ___
We go to a par - ty,   and ev - 'ry - one turns ___
It's time to go home ___ now,   and I've got an ach -

___ to wear. ___   She puts on her make - up
___ to see ___   this beau - ti - ful la - dy
- ing head. ___   So I give her the car ___ keys,

and brush - es her long ___ blonde hair. ___   And then she asks ___
is walk - ing a - round ___ with me. ___   And then she asks ___
and she helps me to bed. ___   And then I tell ___

___ me,   "Do I look all right?" ___   And I say,
___ me,   "Do you feel all right?" ___   And I say,
___ her,   as I turn out light, ___   I say, "My

To Coda ⊕ |¹

"Yes,   you look won - der - ful ___ to - night." ___   (Instrumental)
"Yes,   I feel won - der - ful ___ to - night." ___
dar - ling,   you are won - der - ful ___ to - night ___

THE WRECK OF THE EDMUND FITZGERALD

Words and Music by
GORDON LIGHTFOOT

Additional Lyrics

2. With a load of iron ore twenty-six thousand tons more
    Than the Edmund Fitzgerald weighed empty,
    That good ship and true was a bone to be chewed
    When the gales of November came early.

3. The ship was the pride of the American side
    Coming back from some mill in Wisconsin.
    As the big freighters go, it was bigger than most,
    With a crew and a captain well seasoned.

4. Concluding some terms with a couple of steel firms
    When they left fully loaded for Cleveland.
    And later that night when the ship's bell rang,
    Could it be the north wind they'd been feelin'?

5. The wind in the wires made a tattletale sound
    And a wave broke over the railing.
    And ev'ry man knew, as the captain did too,
    'Twas the witch of November come stealin'.

6. The dawn came late and the breakfast had to wait
    When the gales of November came slashin'.
    When afternoon came, it was freezin' rain
    In the face of a hurricane west wind.

7. When suppertime came, the old cook came on deck
    Sayin', "Fellas, it's too rough to feed ya."
    At seven p.m. a main hatchway caved in
    He said, "Fellas, it's been good to know ya!"

8. The captain wired in he had water comin' in
    And the good ship and crew was in peril.
    And later that night when his lights went outta sight
    Came the wreck of the Edmund Fitzgerald.

9. Does anyone know where the love of God goes
    When the waves turn the minutes to hours?
    The searchers all say they'd have made Whitefish Bay
    If they'd put fifteen more miles behind her.

10. They might have split up or they might have capsized.
    They may have broke deep and took water.
    And all that remains is the faces and the names
    Of the wives and the sons and the daughters.

11. Lake Huron rolls, Superior sings
    In the rooms of her ice-water mansion.
    Old Michigan steams like a young man's dreams;
    The islands and bays are for sportsmen.

12. And farther below, Lake Ontario
    Takes in what Lake Erie can send her.
    And the iron boats go, as the mariners all know,
    With the gales of November remembered.

13. In a musty old hall in Detroit they prayed
    In the Maritime Sailors' Cathedral.
    The church bell chimed till it rang twenty-nine times
    For each man on the Edmund Fitzgerald.

14. The legend lives on from the Chippewa on down
    Of the big lake they call "Gitche Gumee."
    "Superior," they said, "never gives up her dead
    When the gales of November come early."

YOU DIDN'T HAVE TO BE SO NICE

Words and Music by JOHN SEBASTIAN
and STEVE BOONE

Moderately fast

You did-n't have to be so nice. _____
And when we've had a few more days, _____

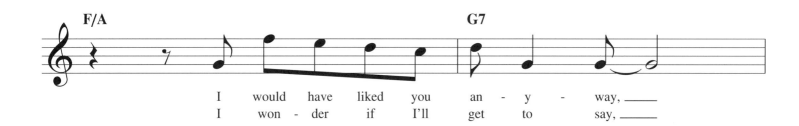

I would have liked you an-y-way, _____
I won-der if I'll get to say, _____

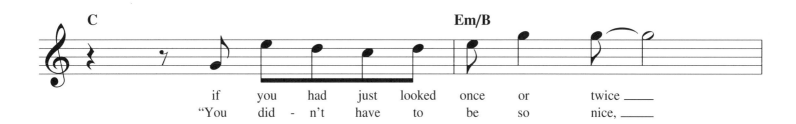

if you had just looked once or twice _____
"You did-n't have to be so nice, _____

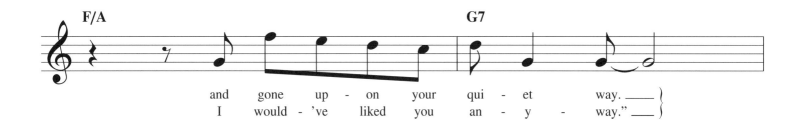

and gone up-on your qui-et way. _____
I would-'ve liked you an-y-way." _____

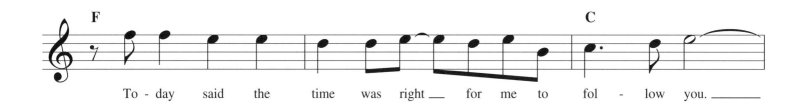

To-day said the time was right ___ for me to fol-low you. _____

_____ I knew I'd find you in a

YOU'RE STILL THE ONE

Words and Music by SHANIA TWAIN
and R.J. LANGE

Moderately slow

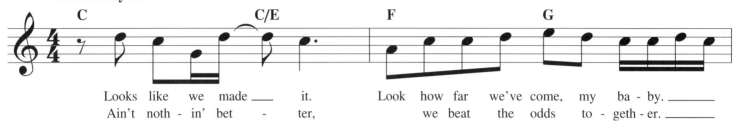

Looks like we made ___ it.   Look how far we've come, my ba - by. _____
Ain't noth - in' bet - ter,   we beat the odds to - geth - er. _____

We might-a took the long ___ way.   We knew we'd get there some day. _____
I'm glad we did - n't lis - ten.   Look at what we would be miss - ing. _____

They said, "I bet   they'll nev - er make it." But just look at us hold - ing on. ___

_____ We're still to - geth - er, still go - ing strong. ___   (You're still the

one.) You're still the one I run to, ___   the one that I be - long to. _____

You're still the one I want for life. (You're still the

one.) You're still the one that I love, ___ the on-ly one I dream of. _____

You're still the one I kiss good - night.

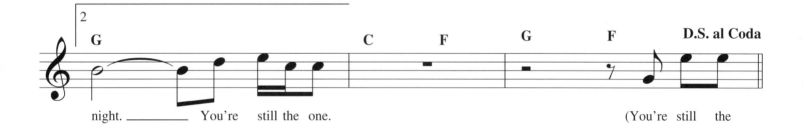

night. _____ You're still the one. (You're still the

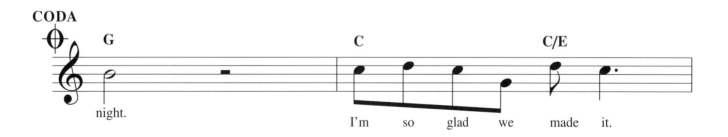

night. I'm so glad we made it.

Look how far we've come, my ba - by. _____

YOUR CHEATIN' HEART

Words and Music by
HANK WILLIAMS

Country Ballad

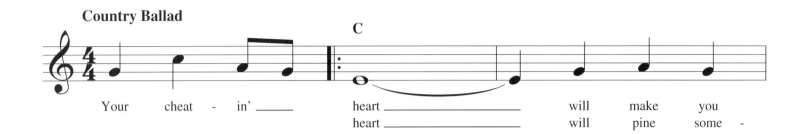

Your cheat - in' _____ heart _____ will make you
heart _____ will pine some -

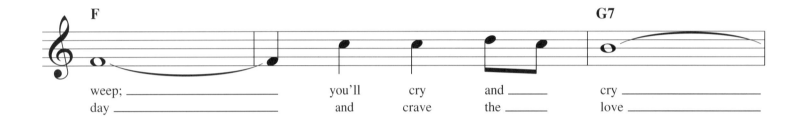

weep; _____ you'll cry and _____ cry _____
day _____ and crave the _____ love _____

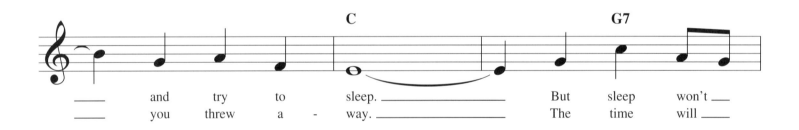

_____ and try to sleep. _____ But sleep won't _____
_____ you threw a - way. _____ The time will _____

come _____ the whole night through. _____
come _____ when you'll be blue. _____

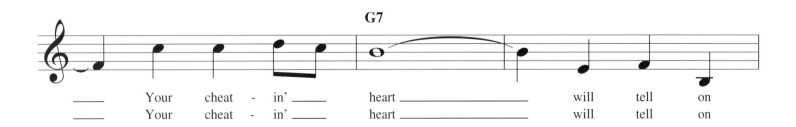

_____ Your cheat - in' _____ heart _____ will tell on
_____ Your cheat - in' _____ heart _____ will tell on

you. _____ } When tears come down _____

____ like fall - in' rain, _____ you'll toss a -

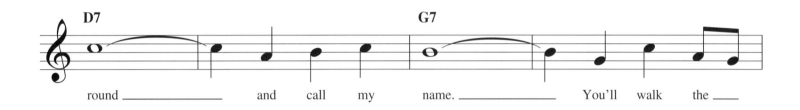

round _____ and call my name. _____ You'll walk the ____

floor _____ the way I do. _____

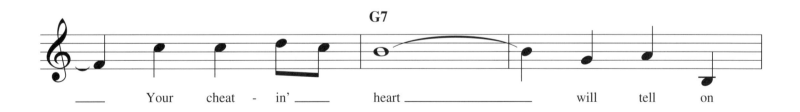

____ Your cheat - in' ____ heart _____ will tell on

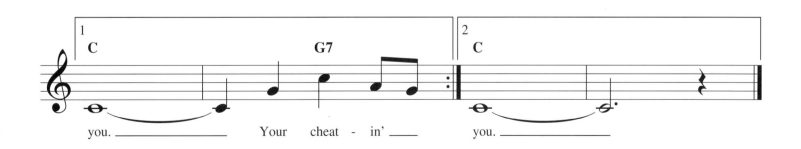

you. _____ Your cheat - in' ____ you. _____

CHORD SPELLER

C chords

C	C–E–G
Cm	C–E♭–G
C7	C–E–G–B♭
Cdim	C–E♭–G♭
C+	C–E–G♯

C♯ or D♭ chords

C♯	C♯–F–G♯
C♯m	C♯–E–G♯
C♯7	C♯–F– G♯–B
C♯dim	C♯–E–G
C♯+	C♯–F–A

D chords

D	D–F♯–A
Dm	D–F–A
D7	D–F♯–A–C
Ddim	D–F–A♭
D+	D–F♯–A♯

E♭ chords

E♭	E♭–G–B♭
E♭m	E♭–G♭–B♭
E♭7	E♭–G–B♭–D♭
E♭dim	E♭–G♭ –A
E♭+	E♭–G–B

E chords

E	E–G♯–B
Em	E–G–B
E7	E–G♯–B–D
Edim	E–G–B♭
E+	E–G♯–C

F chords

F	F–A–C
Fm	F–A♭–C
F7	F–A–C–E♭
Fdim	F–A♭–B
F+	F–A–C♯

F♯ or G♭ chords

F♯	F♯–A♯–C♯
F♯m	F♯–A–C♯
F♯7	F♯–A♯–C♯–E
F♯dim	F♯–A–C
F♯+	F♯–A♯–D

G chords

G	G–B–D
Gm	G–B♭–D
G7	G–B–D–F
Gdim	G–B♭–D♭
G+	G–B–D♯

G♯ or A♭ chords

A♭	A♭–C–E♭
A♭m	A♭–B–E♭
A♭7	A♭–C–E♭–G♭
A♭dim	A♭–B–D
A♭+	A♭–C–E

A chords

A	A–C♯–E
Am	A–C–E
A7	A–C♯–E–G
Adim	A–C–E♭
A+	A–C♯–F

B♭ chords

B♭	B♭–D–F
B♭m	B♭–D♭–F
B♭7	B♭–D–F–A♭
B♭dim	B♭–D♭–E
B♭+	B♭–D–F♯

B chords

B	B–D♯–F♯
Bm	B–D–F♯
B7	B–D♯–F♯–A
Bdim	B–D–F
B+	B–D♯–G

Important Note: A slash chord (C/E, G/B) tells you that a certain bass note is to be played under a particular harmony. In the case of C/E, the chord is C and the bass note is E.

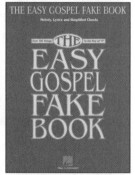

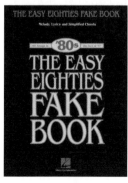
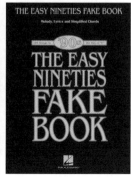
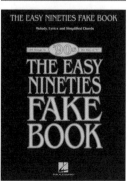

THE ULTIMATE COLLECTION OF
FAKE BOOKS

The Real Book – Sixth Edition
Hal Leonard proudly presents the first legitimate and legal editions of these books ever produced. These bestselling titles are mandatory for anyone who plays jazz! Over 400 songs, including: All By Myself • Dream a Little Dream of Me • God Bless the Child • Like Someone in Love • When I Fall in Love • and more.

00240221   Volume 1, C Edition $35.00
00240224   Volume 1, B♭ Edition $35.00
00240225   Volume 1, E♭ Edition $35.00
00240226   Volume 1, BC Edition................................$35.00
00240222   Volume 2, C Edition $35.00
00240227   Volume 2, B♭ Edition $35.00
00240228   Volume 2, E♭ Edition $35.00

Best Fake Book Ever – 4th Edition
More than 1,000 songs from all styles of music, including: All My Loving • At the Hop • Cabaret • Dust in the Wind • Fever • From a Distance • Hello, Dolly! • Hey Jude • King of the Road • Longer • Misty • Route 66 • Sentimental Journey • Somebody • Song Sung Blue • Spinning Wheel • Unchained Melody • We Will Rock You • What a Wonderful World • Wooly Bully • Y.M.C.A. • and more.

00290239   C Edition $49.99
00240083   B♭ Edition $49.95
00240084   E♭ Edition $49.95

Classic Rock Fake Book – 2nd Edition
This fake book is a great compilation of more than 250 terrific songs of the rock era, arranged for piano, voice, guitar and all C instruments. Includes: All Right Now • American Woman • Birthday • Honesty • I Shot the Sheriff • I Want You to Want Me • Imagine • It's Still Rock and Roll to Me • Lay Down Sally • Layla • My Generation • Rock and Roll All Nite • Spinning Wheel • White Room • We Will Rock You • lots more!
00240108 ....$32.50

Classical Fake Book – 2nd Edition
This unprecedented, amazingly comprehensive reference includes over 850 classical themes and melodies for all classical music lovers. Includes everything from Renaissance music to Vivaldi and Mozart to Mendelssohn. Lyrics in the original language are included when appropriate.
00240044 ....$37.50

The Disney Fake Book – 3rd Edition
Over 200 of the most beloved songs of all time, including: Be Our Guest • Can You Feel the Love Tonight • Colors of the Wind • Cruella De Vil • Friend Like Me • Heigh-Ho • It's a Small World • Mickey Mouse March • Supercalifragilisticexpialidocious • Under the Sea • When You Wish upon a Star • A Whole New World • Zip-A-Dee-Doo-Dah • and more!
00240039 ....$30.00

(Disney characters and artwork © Disney Enterprises, Inc.)

The Folksong Fake Book
Over 1,000 folksongs perfect for performers, school teachers, and hobbyists. Includes: Bury Me Not on the Lone Prairie • Clementine • Danny Boy • The Erie Canal • Go, Tell It on the Mountain • Home on the Range • Kumbaya • Michael Row the Boat Ashore • Shenandoah • Simple Gifts • Swing Low, Sweet Chariot • When Johnny Comes Marching Home • Yankee Doodle • and many more.
00240151 ....$24.95

The Hymn Fake Book
Nearly 1,000 multi-denominational hymns perfect for church musicians or hobbyists: Amazing Grace • Christ the Lord Is Risen Today • For the Beauty of the Earth • It Is Well with My Soul • A Mighty Fortress Is Our God • O for a Thousand Tongues to Sing • Praise to the Lord, the Almighty • Take My Life and Let It Be • What a Friend We Have in Jesus • and hundreds more!
00240145 ....$24.95

The Praise & Worship Fake Book
400 songs: As the Deer • Better Is One Day • Come, Now Is the Time to Worship • Firm Foundation • Glorify Thy Name • Here I Am to Worship • I Could Sing of Your Love Forever • Lord, I Lift Your Name on High • More Precious Than Silver • Open the Eyes of My Heart • The Power of Your Love • Shine, Jesus, Shine • Trading My Sorrows • We Fall Down • You Are My All in All • and more.
00240234..$34.95

The R&B Fake Book – 2nd Edition
This terrific fake book features 375 classic R&B hits: Baby Love • Best of My Love • Dancing in the Street • Easy • Get Ready • Heatwave • Here and Now • Just Once • Let's Get It On • The Loco-Motion • (You Make Me Feel Like) A Natural Woman • One Sweet Day • Papa Was a Rollin' Stone • Save the Best for Last • September • Sexual Healing • Shop Around • Still • Tell It Like It Is • Up on the Roof • Walk on By • What's Going On • more!
00240107   C Edition $29.95

Ultimate Broadway Fake Book – 5th Edition
More than 700 show-stoppers from over 200 shows! Includes: Ain't Misbehavin' • All I Ask of You • Bewitched • Camelot • Don't Cry for Me Argentina • Edelweiss • I Dreamed a Dream • If I Were a Rich Man • Memory • Oklahoma • Send in the Clowns • What I Did for Love • more.
00240046..$49.99

FOR MORE INFORMATION, SEE YOUR LOCAL MUSIC DEALER, OR WRITE TO:

7777 W. BLUEMOUND RD. P.O. BOX 13819 MILWAUKEE, WI 53213

Complete songlists available online at
www.halleonard.com

Prices, contents and availabilty subject to change without notice.

The Ultimate Christmas Fake Book – 5th Edition
This updated edition includes 275 traditional and contemporary Christmas songs: Away in a Manger • The Christmas Song • Deck the Hall • Frosty the Snow Man • A Holly Jolly Christmas • I Heard the Bells on Christmas Day • Jingle Bells • Little Saint Nick • Merry Christmas, Darling • Nuttin' for Christmas • Rudolph the Red-Nosed Reindeer • Silent Night • What Child Is This? • more.
00240045 ....$24.95

The Ultimate Country Fake Book – 5th Edition
This book includes over 700 of your favorite country hits: Always on My Mind • Boot Scootin' Boogie • Crazy • Down at the Twist and Shout • Forever and Ever, Amen • Friends in Low Places • The Gambler • Jambalaya • King of the Road • Sixteen Tons • There's a Tear in My Beer • Your Cheatin' Heart • and hundreds more.
00240049 ....$49.99

The Ultimate Fake Book – 4th Edition
Includes over 1,200 hits: Blue Skies • Body and Soul • Endless Love • A Foggy Day • Isn't It Romantic? • Memory • Mona Lisa • Moon River • Operator • Piano Man • Roxanne • Satin Doll • Shout • Small World • Speak Softly, Love • Strawberry Fields Forever • Tears in Heaven • Unforgettable • hundreds more!

00240024   C Edition $49.95
00240026   B♭ Edition...$49.95
00240025   E♭ Edition $49.95

The Ultimate Pop/Rock Fake Book – 4th Edition
Over 600 pop standards and contemporary hits, including: All Shook Up • Another One Bites the Dust • Crying • Don't Know Much • Dust in the Wind • Earth Angel • Every Breath You Take • Hero • Hey Jude • Hold My Hand • Imagine • Layla • The Loco-Motion • Oh, Pretty Woman • On Broadway • Spinning Wheel • Stand by Me • Stayin' Alive • Tears in Heaven • True Colors • The Twist • Vision of Love • A Whole New World • Wild Thing • Wooly Bully • Yesterday • more!
00240099 ....$39.99

Fake Book of the World's Favorite Songs – 4th Edition
Over 700 favorites, including: America the Beautiful • Anchors Aweigh • Battle Hymn of the Republic • Bill Bailey, Won't You Please Come Home • Chopsticks • Für Elise • His Eye Is on the Sparrow • Jesu, Joy of Man's Desiring • My Old Kentucky Home • Sidewalks of New York • Take Me Out to the Ball Game • When the Saints Go Marching In • and hundreds more!
00240072 ....$22.95

0313

PLAY TODAY® SERIES

THE ULTIMATE SELF-TEACHING SERIES!

How many times have you said: "I wish I would've learned to play guitar… piano… saxophone…" Well, it's time to do something about it. The revolutionary *Play Today!* Series from Hal Leonard will get you doing what you've always wanted to do: make music. Best of all, with these book/CD packs you can listen and learn at your own pace, in the comfort of your own home! This method can be used by students who want to teach themselves or by teachers for private or group instruction. It is a complete guide to the basics, designed to offer quality instruction in the book and on the CD, terrific songs, and a professional-quality CD with tons of full-demo tracks and audio instruction. Each book includes over 70 great songs and examples!

Play Accordion Today!
00701744	Level 1 Book/CD Pack	$9.99
00702657	Level 1 Songbook Book/CD Pack	$12.99

Play Alto Sax Today! *DVD CD*
00842049	Level 1 Book/CD Pack	$9.95
00842050	Level 2 Book/CD Pack	$9.95
00320359	DVD	$14.95
00842051	Songbook Book/CD Pack	$12.95
00699555	Beginner's Pack – Level 1 Book/CD & DVD	$19.95
00699492	Play Today Plus Book/CD Pack	$14.95

Play Banjo Today!
00699897	Level 1 Book/CD Pack	$9.95
00701006	Level 2 Book/CD Pack	$9.99
00320913	DVD	$14.99
00701873	Beginner's Pack – Level 1 Book/CD & DVD	$19.95

Play Bass Today! *DVD CD INCLUDES TAB*
00842020	Level 1 Book/CD Pack	$9.95
00842036	Level 2 Book/CD Pack	$9.95
00320356	DVD	$14.95
00842037	Songbook Book/CD Pack	$12.95
00699552	Beginner's Pack – Level 1 Book/CD & DVD	$19.95
00698997	Play Today Plus Book/CD Pack	$14.95

Play Clarinet Today! *DVD CD*
00842046	Level 1 Book/CD Pack	$9.95
00842047	Level 2 Book/CD Pack	$9.95
00320358	DVD	$14.95
00842048	Songbook Book/CD Pack	$12.95
00699554	Beginner's Pack – Level 1 Book/CD & DVD	$19.95
00699490	Play Today Plus Book/CD Pack	$14.95

Play Dobro® Today!
00701505	Level 1 Book/CD Pack	$9.99

Play Drums Today! *DVD CD*
00842021	Level 1 Book/CD Pack	$9.95
00842038	Level 2 Book/CD Pack	$9.95
00320355	DVD	$14.95
00842039	Songbook Book/CD Pack	$12.95
00699551	Beginner's Pack – Level 1 Book/CD & DVD	$19.95
00699001	Play Today Plus Book/CD Pack	$14.95

Play Flute Today! *DVD CD*
00842043	Level 1 Book/CD Pack	$9.95
00842044	Level 2 Book/CD Pack	$9.95
00320360	DVD	$14.95
00842045	Songbook Book/CD Pack	$12.95
00699553	Beginner's Pack – Level 1 Book/CD & DVD	$19.95
00699489	Play Today Plus Book/CD Pack	$14.95

Play Guitar Today! *DVD CD INCLUDES TAB*
00696100	Level 1 Book/CD Pack	$9.99
00696101	Level 2 Book/CD Pack	$9.95
00320353	DVD	$14.95
00696102	Songbook Book/CD Pack	$12.95
00699544	Beginner's Pack – Level 1 Book/CD & DVD	$19.95
00842055	Play Today Plus Book/CD Pack	$14.95
00702431	Worship Songbook Book/CD Pack	$12.99
00695662	Complete Kit	$29.95

Play Harmonica Today!
00700179	Level 1 Book/CD Pack	$9.99
00320653	DVD	$14.99
00701875	Beginner's Pack – Level 1 Book/CD & DVD	$19.95

Play Mandolin Today!
00699911	Level 1 Book/CD Pack	$9.99
00320909	DVD	$14.99
00701874	Beginner's Pack – Level 1 Book/CD & DVD	$19.95

Play Piano Today! *DVD CD*
00842019	Level 1 Book/CD Pack	$9.99
00842040	Level 2 Book/CD Pack	$9.95
00320354	DVD	$14.95
00842041	Songbook Book/CD Pack	$12.95
00699545	Beginner's Pack – Level 1 Book/CD & DVD	$19.95
00699044	Play Today Plus Book/CD Pack	$14.95
00702415	Worship Songbook Book/CD Pack	$12.99

Play Recorder Today! *CD*
00700919	Level 1 Book/CD Pack	$7.95
00701245	Songbook Book CD/Pack	$12.99

Sing Today! *CD*
00699761	Level 1 Book/CD Pack	$9.95

Play Trombone Today! *DVD CD*
00699917	Level 1 Book/CD Pack	$9.95
00320508	DVD	$14.99

Play Trumpet Today! *DVD CD*
00842052	Level 1 Book/CD Pack	$9.95
00842053	Level 2 Book/CD Pack	$9.95
00320357	DVD	$14.95
00842054	Songbook Book/CD Pack	$12.95
00699556	Beginner's Pack – Level 1 Book/CD & DVD	$19.95
00699491	Play Today Plus Book/CD Pack	$14.95

Play Ukulele Today! *CD*
00699638	Level 1 Book/CD Pack	$9.99
00699655	Play Today Plus Book/CD Pack	$9.95
00320985	DVD	$14.99
00701872	Beginner's Pack – Level 1 Book/CD & DVD	$19.95
00650743	Book/CD/DVD with Ukulele	$39.99
00701002	Level 2 Book/CD Pack	$9.99
00702484	Level 2 Songbook Book/CD Pack	$12.99

Play Violin Today! *CD*
00699748	Level 1 Book/CD Pack	$9.95
00701320	Level 2 Book/CD Pack	$9.99
00321076	DVD	$14.99
00701700	Songbook Book/CD Pack	$12.99
00701876	Beginner's Pack – Level 1 Book/CD & DVD	$19.95

HAL•LEONARD® CORPORATION

7777 W. BLUEMOUND RD. P.O. BOX 13819 MILWAUKEE, WI 53213

Visit us online at **www.halleonard.com**

Prices, contents and availability subject to change without notice.

0613